OXFORD WORLD'S CLASSICS

JOHANN WOLFGANG GOETHE

The Flight to Italy

Diary and Selected Letters

Edited and translated with an Introduction by
T. J. REED

OXFORD
UNIVERSITY PRESS

OXFORD
UNIVERSITY PRESS

Great Clarendon Street, Oxford OX2 6DP

Oxford University Press is a department of the University of Oxford
It furthers the University's objective of excellence in research, scholarship,
and education by publishing worldwide in

Oxford New York

Athens Auckland Bangkok Bogotá Buenos Aires Calcutta
Cape Town Chennai Dar es Salaam Delhi Florence Hong Kong Istanbul
Karachi Kuala Lumpur Madrid Melbourne Mexico City Mumbai
Nairobi Paris São Paulo Singapore Taipei Tokyo Toronto Warsaw

with associated companies in Berlin Ibadan

Oxford is a registered trade mark of Oxford University Press
in the UK and in certain other countries

Published in the United States
by Oxford University Press Inc., New York

British Library Cataloguing in Publication Data
Data available

Library of Congress Cataloging in Publication Data
Data available

ISBN 0–19–283886–5

1 3 5 7 9 10 8 6 4 2

Typeset in Ehrhardt
by RefineCatch Limited, Bungay, Suffolk
Printed in Great Britain by
Cox & Wyman Ltd., Reading, Berkshire

For David Constantine

CONTENTS

ACKNOWLEDGEMENTS

THE breadth of Goethe's interests meant I needed advice on wording, and at times help in understanding what Goethe was driving at, in matters of architecture, art history, botany, economics, geology, meteorology, and things Italian. For expertise kindly made available I am grateful to Sir Howard Colvin, Nicholas Dimsdale, Martin Frank, Polly Gray, Peter Hainsworth, Jane Langdale, and Fred Taylor. Any errors in these matters remain mine.

INTRODUCTION

I

IN the small hours of 3 September 1786 a writer, a courtier, an administrator, a natural scientist, and an artist left Carlsbad for Italy. They were not a party, but a single man: Johann Wolfgang Goethe, destined within his lifetime and ever since to be the central figure in Germany's culture, but now at the age of 37 frustrated and divided against himself, overworked yet under-achieving, disillusioned by his failure to reform the administration of one of Germany's many petty states, painfully aware of a backlog of literary works he had begun but not finished, embroiled in a bizarre and increasingly difficult relationship with a married court lady seven years his senior, and—probably as a consequence of all this—suffering from some kind of psychosomatic illness or depression which the gloom of northern skies further intensified. Reason enough to want a break. But that early-morning departure was a positive escape—'they wouldn't have let me go if I hadn't'—and he was to stay away almost two years, turning the break into one of the shaping experiences of his life.

Many years later Goethe published a full and formal account of it called *Italian Journey*, drawing on jottings and letters written at the time, but rearranging, cutting and adding, shifting the perspective and altering the tone. So the authentic feel of his Italian experience is best captured in his diary of the first eight weeks, the time it took him to get to Rome. The essentials of the journey are all there. Goethe himself had no high opinion of this little document, and it is a wonder he never destroyed it as he did many of his other papers once they had helped him construct his mature retrospect. Yet if writing is the imprint of personality, the diary is a book in its own right, all the more so for being informal, colloquial, impressionistic, under-punctuated, unpolished, with loose ends showing and changes of mind not tidied away. It is Goethe in shirtsleeves, moving not posing. For readers with a taste for spontaneity it is a delightfully zestful book, by a poet who has few equals in the ability to celebrate ordinary experience and convey happiness as a necessary and convincing theme. And since it is a record of restored vitality and new beginnings, it makes an excellent antidote to the cliché view of Goethe as an elderly exponent of settled wisdom.

Who were 'they' who 'wouldn't have let him go', and what kind of hold did they have on him? Most immediately, Goethe was leaving behind him a group from the court of Saxe-Weimar, his employer and friend the Duke among them, who had been taking the waters at that Bohemian spa. Beyond them it was the society of the duchy generally, the nobility and gentry among whom he was now accepted, the administrators with whom he worked, and ultimately the 100,000 souls who lived in this miniature state. Their needs had occupied his mind and taken up a lot of his time and energy since 1775, when Carl August (aged 18) brought him to Weimar and promptly set him up, not as court poet but (to the shock of the grey-headed establishment—Goethe was only 26) as a member of the Privy Council and three of its administrative departments: roads, mines, the army. Goethe was a trained lawyer, and to that extent fitted for this kind of work. Later on he was given the special task of disentangling the affairs of the exchequer.

The scale of these responsibilities did not make him a politician, much less a statesman. The army was a few hundred men; a handful more were recruited every three years, and Goethe was routinely present when they were mustered and measured. The only remotely 'political' problem was how to limit the activities of Prussia's recruiting officers on Weimar soil without affronting Frederick the Great. Likewise, roads had a small budget that allowed patching but no serious rebuilding. There could be no grand scheme, if only because in a small territory like Weimar any major route was just passing through and became some other ruler's responsibility a mile or two further on. Yet precisely the small scale of Goethe's duties and the personal involvement it led to had benefits for a poet whose highly charged imagination had nurtured visions of Promethean defiance and Faustian aspiration. Almost literally, it earthed his emotional energies.

But there could be too much of that particular good thing. By the mid-eighties Goethe felt his energies were not so much earthed as squashed. He badly needed to restore what he called 'the elasticity of my spirit'. In the private sphere, his intense yet not physical relationship with Charlotte von Stein[1] was now so fraught that absence seemed the only way to make the heart grow fonder. Distance, he wrote (though without saying where from), would give her more than his presence often had.[2] Specifically it would give her this diary, which he wrote as something between journal entries and letters, and sent in five successive bundles from different points on his route. As for his baulked creativity, on his birthday at Carlsbad on 28 August friends sent him greetings as from various unfinished works—*Faust* perhaps, *Egmont*, *Torquato Tasso*, *Wilhelm Meister?*—asking why he had not completed them, a joke that would surely have been the last straw if his journey had not already been a settled thing.

   Settled and also carefully prepared: Goethe had put his administrative affairs in order and left his trusted servant Seidel with instructions on what to do and what to tell people. He wanted his administrative subordinates, for obvious reasons, to expect his return any day. Nobody was to know where he had gone: he would tell them in his own good time. Nor was anyone along his route to know who he was: he took a cover-name, one so common (Möller) that it hardly made an identity at all. He thus vanished from home without becoming visible anywhere else. If 1786 was an identity crisis, then not because Goethe was uncertain who he was; rather, he was certain who and what he no longer wanted to be.

   The result was a way of journeying unusual for the time. The normal practice and safeguard for people of consequence in a foreign land was to travel in style, with letters of introduction that enabled you to enjoy the freemasonry of rank. You hired your own vehicle, as Gibbon had for his Italian trip in 1764. Goethe did the opposite of all this. He travelled by any and every kind of public transport and stayed wherever it stopped. He took no servant with him and felt the more human for it. He deliberately downgraded his dress—one wonders quite what was so socially lowering about those linen 'netherstocks' (p. 50)—and once well into Italy he dressed more like an Italian, tried to copy the gestures he observed, and did his best to melt into the background. He met and talked to all sorts and conditions of men, and some women too—he plainly had the common touch. He refrained from commissioning a picture of a building he especially liked because so lordly a gesture would have blown his

---

   [1] On whom see below, 'Goethe's Circle and Correspondents', p. 156.
   [2] To Charlotte, 18 Sept. 1786.

cover. It is true he paid calls on known naturalists or art-collectors, but without fanfare and as far as we can tell without resorting to his real name. And he did have quite a name. He was the author of one of the century's most sensational novels, *The Sufferings of Young Werther*, and of several dramas. He had already made a notable scientific discovery, that human beings did after all have vestiges of the intermaxillary bone previously thought to be present only in animals. He was a prominent figure in the government of a German state—admittedly a small one, but not so small that it did not have some role in the manœuvrings of eighteenth-century politics. (When Austrian agents in Rome discovered who Goethe was, they assumed he was on a diplomatic mission to the Pope.) Altogether he had a good deal of identity to conceal.

Concealing it was no doubt part of the pleasure of release, the holiday mood. On the one occasion when he was recognized, he took a mischievous delight in denying who he was. But there was a deeper logic too. He was travelling to feel the grain of reality again—in the words of another traveller, 'to come down off the featherbed of civilisation and find the globe granite underfoot and strewn with cutting flints'.[3] He wanted to be unburdened by duties, untrammelled by etiquette, not aided or impeded by an entourage, not influenced by common or guidebook opinion, but left to his own devices, all in the cause of seeing with his own eyes: 'what I'm after now is the sense impressions that no book and no picture can give me, so that I start to take an interest in the world again'. A world of perceptions then, not descriptions; of things, not words. Not because words are unimportant to a writer, but because they need a reality to back them, as any paper currency does. And perceiving things truly, or in Goethe's favourite word 'purely', needed a fresh, unprejudiced observer. Making a new start in outward things was part of the process of turning himself into this necessary instrument. His escape, his incognito, his abandoning of rank were in all seriousness what Philip Larkin's poem 'Poetry of Departures' ironically calls an 'audacious, purifying, elemental move';[4] and giving up his own name was the ultimate symbolic farewell to an old order of words. Only when safely in Rome did he stick the personal label back on again—

[3] Robert Louis Stevenson, *Travels with a Donkey in the Cévennes*, in the chapter 'Cheylard and Luc'.
[4] In the collection *The Less Deceived* (Marvell Press, 1955) 34.

but by now on an already changed person—when he greeted his future friend and mentor, the painter Tischbein, with a simple 'I am Goethe'.

Yet human slates cannot be wiped completely clean. Much of what Goethe had become by 1786, some of the fugitive's many functions and the experience they had brought him, would be vital to the new enterprise. He knows from the start that he has his own 'way of seeing', and he consciously enjoys it. He may have chosen to slough off his administrator's rank, but he still sees things with an administrator's eye. Or with the exact eye of a scientist. Or with the pictorial eye of a graphic artist. The administrator sizes up the way towns are located at the focal points of geographical, economic, and social forces; the different speed of progress and frequency of potholes on Bavarian as against Bohemian roads are registered by bones that have sat through Roads Commission meetings and paced out the stretches of Weimar surface that needed repair. The running of Italian polities—Tuscany good, the Papal State bad—is likewise observed with a practitioner's eye. He finds the streets of Venice strewn with refuse, and devises a plan to keep them clean as he goes along. The geologist for his part not only chips off specimens of rock everywhere (a habit he had meant to break); he consciously travels over the shape of the continent, crossing the great ranges that make nations, watersheds, and the weather. Weather is itself not just a local circumstance of the day's journeying. The amateur meteorologist consciously drops down through the latitudes and moves through the larger weather-system, watching the mountains brew storms for his friends back home even as he enjoys the Italian sunshine. And when Goethe notes the local people's facial structure and physique, their diet and state of health, their behaviour as a society, the patterns of their culture in the broadest sense, is that the administrator thinking of their welfare? Or the scientist analysing physical cause and effect? Or the artist practising his eye for human distinctiveness? Or have all these interests merged in the all-embracing anthropology that eighteenth-century writers felt they were ultimately contributing to?

However we categorize what Goethe observed, everything is concrete and immediate, everything has a ground of experience within a framework of reflection. He no sooner sees than he connects; if he doesn't know, he enquires, wonders, speculates, sketches a quick theory, but always with the open mind of an undogmatic empiricist:

'here's an opinion that needs to be tested'; 'this needs a follow-up study'; 'as you know, I'm not a specialist'; 'I still can't work out what goes on'; 'I have a notion, I won't put it any higher than that'; 'I haven't yet been given a full account.' Not surprisingly, some of his hypotheses now seem more quaint than cogent: the 'elasticity of the air' as a maker of the weather makes no sense to an atmospheric physicist, though Goethe was right to look so closely at what went on around mountains. But if he was wrong in some of his dashed-off theories, at least he was actively pursuing a greater range of disparate enquiries at the same time than any one modern head normally carries. Some of his theories may yet turn out to be right; his botanical intuitions are proving to be hardy perennials. At all events, Goethe hardly needed the advice an Italian fellow-passenger gave him near the end of his journey: don't concentrate on one thing, it will drive you mad, you need a thousand things, a confusion of things in your head. He also knew his own limitations, of knowledge in science, of ability in drawing and painting. It is not false modesty when he says that the real point of all his interests is that they open up the world to him.

For whatever the 'objective' rightness of Goethe's ideas, he had in another sense of the word an objective mind, a mind that was drawn to the world of objects and devoted to seeing them as exactly as he could because they were what finally constituted truth and validated art. Far from being aridly reductive, it was an emotional attraction too, even a secularized religious devotion. His favourite philosopher was Spinoza, who had said that the more we understand individual things, the more we understand God.[5] This meant confronting and transfiguring the everyday, as programmatically set out in some lines he sent to his friend Merck with a portfolio of his drawings in 1774:

> God grant that you may love your shoe,
> Every deformed potato too,
> Try to see each object plain,
> Its peace and power, joy and pain,
> And feel the whole world's held in place
> By the high heavens' grand embrace.

Only then, he concludes, will you be a true artist.

---

[5] *Ethics*, Part 5, Proposition xxv, Everyman ed. T. S. Gregory, London, 1963, 214. Cf. Goethe's letters to F. H. Jacobi of 9 June 1785 and 5 May 1786.

If Goethe as scientist, poet, and artist saw the phenomenal world with a loving eye, the world seemed mysteriously to respond. In a recurrent turn of phrase, the objects he observes and tries to understand are not inert, they 'come to meet him' or 'rise to meet him', they 'show him their nature'. It is as if they cannot wait to be taken in by so appreciative an observer. Looking back years later he summed up this mutuality, again in lines accompanying a set of drawings:

> I saw the world and love was in my sight,
> And world and I, we revelled in delight.

That warmth of feeling informs even his soberest descriptions, and sometimes it breaks out in exuberant delight at the sheer fact and feel of a live thing's existing, as when little crabs on the beach at Venice give him 'a glow of pleasure' because they are 'so matched to their condition, so true, so *being*!'

Besides this rich and zestful way of seeing that Goethe took with him to Italy, he had expectations *about* Italy which equally meant that he was by no means starting with a clean slate. Though he travelled incognito, he was not heading for *terra incognita*. Landscape and ancient remains, links with Classical literature, cities filled with the art and architecture of the Renaissance, all this made Italy the fundamental European culture, a source of multiple authority, a necessary part of any full education and cultivation. Rabelais had been there, Montaigne had been there, Dürer had been there—most importantly for Goethe, his father had been there. His expectations were thus intimate psychological ones, not just cultural generalities. The tales Johann Caspar Goethe told, the travel diary he had written (in Italian), the Italian views that hung in the hall, the model gondola he brought back from Venice with him, had planted a seed of desire in the child which by 1786 had grown into an obsession. The grown man had twice looked down on Italy from a Swiss pass and turned back. Italy was the Promised Land, a destined fulfilment—Goethe had a powerful sense of personal destiny—but it needed the right moment. The first lines of his diary declare with simple solemnity that this moment has come: 'for it was time.'

Images abound for what Goethe felt happening to him on the road to Rome and during his Italian stay: in the Christian metaphor, it was a new life, in a specifically Pietist one a rebirth; it was a transfiguration of the self; it was a revolution within him; it was a return to a

warm and welcoming homeland from a voyage in Arctic seas. The
first word from Rome to his Weimar friends[6] uses the myth of Pygmalion to express a threefold delight at the way his dreams and
perceptions have come true, come together, and come alive, much as
the sculptor's beautiful statue came alive and came towards him, a
woman now of flesh and blood.

All this heightened language suggests that Goethe was carrying
his emotional fulfilment with him to Italy. Certainly a potential was
there to be released. Yet he also insists he is maintaining a deliberate
calm so that any heightened mood must be the effect of the objects
seen, not of a pre-emptive imagination. Entry after entry talks of
looking long and hard, of looking repeatedly at the same things, of
acquiring and possessing images, of seeing in his own way and forming his own judgement. In this Goethe was being true to the classic
Enlightenment precept that people should see and think for themselves. But more often than not this had meant looking sceptically,
seeing *through* things—old beliefs, prejudices, practices—in the
cause of human liberation and new beginnings. Goethe's seeing is,
with one significant exception, wholly affirmative. Objectivity
engenders enthusiasm. Given the right match of mind and matter
why should it not?

II

What exactly did Goethe see and what did he make of it? First there
were the mountain and valley landscapes as he crossed the Alps, the
'finest sights of nature' as a prelude to Antiquity and culture. Then
before he ever set eyes on an ancient monument or a work of art,
there was the live Italian present, the vitality and constant bustling
activity of the populace, their easygoing way of life, the openness and
joviality that seemed to come from living in the open air, which in
turn was all the southern climate's doing. Climate is the revelation
that underlies all else. When he packs his overcoat away just before
Verona—'it isn't exactly hot, but you feel warm really deep inside
you, in a way that for ages I haven't had any conception of'—he is
talking about far more than a physical sensation; and when he tells
Charlotte that she too would feel well in this climate, or that he

---

[6] See Letter 1 in this volume.

wishes he could bring a piece of it back home with him, what he is really talking about is the psychic climate of mood and mindset. And when he actually calls climate the only thing that gives Italy the edge over home, he is partly playing down all the other things Italy offers because he suspects that too frank an enjoyment will aggravate in her eyes the original offence of absconding. But he is also implying more than he consciously means to: that Germany, far up in the north with its unalterable climate, will never be able to make him as happy as he is now; nor, unless the personal climate changes, will she. As it proved: his return only completed the split his departure had opened up.

Goethe's other enjoyments are cultural, but not in the manner of a tourist ticking off the obligatory sights. That, he later says in a letter from Rome, is enviably easy compared with the work of serious seeing. In Verona he experiences his first ancient monument, the amphitheatre, but on his way back he comes upon a ball-game where the contemporary crowd has naturally disposed itself in the identical bowl shape of the ancient arena. To Goethe's eye for origins and process, ancient and modern join in a single vision; architecture is the shaping in stone of human impulse and need. On a larger scale, he reads Venice in the same evolutionary way as an organic growth from the most bizarre conditions, restricted space, marshy terrain, infiltration by the tides. Architecture also provides the central artist-hero of the diary and Goethe's biggest artistic experience before Rome—he presents it as an almost mystical revelation that goes beyond art into life—namely, the sixteenth-century architect Andrea Palladio and his buildings at Vicenza and Venice. Works of the Renaissance then, not of Antiquity, but true to Antiquity in a way Renaissance painting, with its overwhelmingly Christian subjects, decidedly was not. Palladio's splendid villas raised no doctrinal problems; but when he was commissioned to design new churches or add to existing ones, Antiquity and Christianity came into conflict. Palladio followed ancient precepts, at whatever risk of dissonance with standard forms and Christian beliefs. Goethe imagines him weighing the risks—before proceeding undaunted. For Palladio, he says, had absorbed too much of the existence of the ancients to be ready to accept the littleness and narrowness of the time in which he was born without trying to reshape it to his own noble conceptions. That was the situation and mission of any European Classicist committed to more than mere surface decoration. Goethe was writing the job-description for a new phase in his own work, and perhaps he knew it.

Aesthetics and ideology mingle from Goethe's very first response to an ancient work of art, a sarcophagus with carvings that confront death by gently commemorating life. They portray everyday human actions and affections, and thus assert 'the simple present of human beings' in such a way that 'their existence is continued and made permanent'. The point would be clear enough by itself, but Goethe draws the contrast with a piece of Christian tomb art, where a knight is on his knees praying for future resurrection. It is not just that Goethe was 'a decided non-Christian'.[7] His appreciation and his criticism are both equally rooted in the nature of the visual medium. Painting and carving are arts of physical presence, of objects and figures re-presented in picture or stone, not of things imagined somewhere outside them. The work of art stands or falls by what we see. This insistence on visible things in their own right explains Goethe's revulsion at much of the Christian art that was now all round him. For what were depictions of torture and martyrdom and crucifixion in their own right? Mere gratuitous horror, if the transcendent purpose and heavenly reward were left out of account—as in pictorial terms they were bound to be. That is what 'transcendent' means: beyond the earthly and hence necessarily outside the physical reach of any picture or sculpture. True, the promised bliss of heaven could have been made into a visual subject, but it is one that painters rarely took up, no doubt because it was hard to do it justice and perhaps hubris to try. Torment and sacrifice were an easy option. Goethe's rejection becomes at times a bitter fury.

But not towards the artists. It was not their fault. They were merely the instruments of their society and its beliefs, and Goethe's heart goes out to them for the way their art was denatured by the orthodoxy that commissioned it. Occasionally, to Goethe's pleasure, they managed to escape from doctrinal constriction into free human space: a Christ-child pulls a frightened little face at the adoring Magi; a Virgin suckles her child in puzzlement as if it were a changeling, unaware of the larger story she has become part of; Christ after the crucifixion bears all the signs of a suffering that resurrection has

[7] Letter to Johann Caspar Lavater, 29 July 1782.

not healed; an Assumption of the Virgin shows her looking not up to heaven but back down at her earthly friends.

But these are rare details. Otherwise Goethe can only admire the painters' technical skills, separating them as far as is feasible from the imposed ends. One comment, 'a senseless conception carried through with absolute genius', puts his view in a nutshell. He connects early masters like Mantegna—an extraordinary scatter-shot of adjectives tries to encompass the qualities of his primal real-ism—backwards to Antiquity and forwards to Titian and Raphael in a tradition of technical development independent of subject-matter. Raphael he links with Palladio as possessing absolute greatness, though for different reasons. He is the one painter whose genius transcends transcendence through a perfection that restores the image to self-sufficiency: 'Five saints side by side, none of whom are of any concern to us, but whose existence is so perfect that one wishes the picture may last forever, though content with one's own dissolution.' A humanist can hardly say fairer than that.

Once Goethe is in Rome, and later during his trip to Naples and Sicily, the balance shifts away from Renaissance art back to the works of Antiquity. He studies and draws under the guidance of Tischbein and the other artists of their small colony, and above all he goes on avidly seeing. He fills his mind with 'solid' buildings and statuary, making it sound as if he were physically packing them into his head. Conversely, the solidity he keeps talking about is not just a quality of the physical world, it pervades the observer's whole being, he feels himself *becoming* 'solid'. Exactly what this means and how it oper-ated, indeed how exactly the whole Italian experience worked on Goethe to restore and transform him, is ultimately not fathomable. But his diary and letters of the time convey the sustained excitement and happiness of feeling it happen. That is their attraction. A great personality takes on a new lease of life before our eyes.

III

In her typically warm and shrewd response to the news that her son was in Italy, Goethe's mother foretold the lifelong benefits his journey would bring.[8] As his stay developed, it seemed to promise

[8] See Letter 4.

the same: it was a two-year idyll, not of relaxed leisure but intense activity, gathering material, storing sights and insights, renewing energies—all long-term investments for his future work. He uses that metaphor himself,[9] alongside the more elevated ones of rebirth and a new life. But for a time it looked as if all the gains might be wasted. The happiness of being in paradise was equalled by the misery of being expelled from it and the disillusionment of coming back to Germany. The climate, literal and metaphorical, was unwelcoming. 'The weather is very gloomy all the time and kills my spirits; when the barometer is down and the landscape has no colour, how is it possible to live?'—this to Herder,[10] who had now gone off to Italy himself in the entourage of the Dowager Duchess. Goethe had declined a pressing invitation to go with them, having only just returned to—and, as he saw it, for the benefit of—his friends. But the friends seemed indifferent. Weimar society had no sense of his profound renewal; in their eyes, he had merely taken Italian leave. Relations with Charlotte in particular were bad. She was cool and reproachful, she put him on the defensive, all cordiality was gone. He told her she was ruining her nerves with too much coffee. But her irritability was also caused by a different chemistry. Goethe had taken a mistress to live with him, Christiane Vulpius, a younger, less educated, less complicated woman who (as he pointed out) claimed and reciprocated feelings of a kind Charlotte never had. So who was the loser?[11] That made no difference to the logic of Charlotte's possessiveness. But it made an immense difference to Goethe's poetry. And in an extraordinary way, the new love matched and began to set free the stored potential of his Italian time.

In those two years Goethe the creative writer had been virtually silent. He had written only two new poems. Even in his diary and letters he often cut short descriptions with a 'more when we meet', and the like. The later letters from Rome, Herder complained, were like dishes with no food in them.[12] Goethe was of course busy in Italy revising earlier works for a forthcoming collected edition, a practical reason for literary silence. But there was an intrinsic reason too, connected with his pursuit of sense impressions and that packing in

---

[9]   See Letter 22.
[10] Letter of 2 or 3 Sept. 1788.
[11] Letter of 1 June 1789.
[12] Reported in Goethe's letter to Christian Gottlieb Heyne, 24 July 1788.

of the solid objects Rome offered. After a good day of looking, he writes that there is little he can actually *say*, indeed the right thing is to maintain a discipline of silence. 'I could stay here for years without saying much,' he goes on. It has all been so thoroughly described and analysed, what matters is to open your eyes and study it.[13] The implication is that in the face of such solid reality words are premature or presumptuous, would block perception or perhaps squander the substance that seeing and study have accumulated.

But it was not just guidebook description that Goethe was averse to. Higher forms of writing could also obscure the solidity of the object-world, or fail to approach it at all, by interposing veils of feeling and imagination. Modern literature wrung poetic poignancy from the loss of that contact and turned direct desire into the subtle emotion of yearning. In a brilliant overview of ancient and modern literature, Goethe's future ally Friedrich Schiller was to declare in 1795 that such secondary feelings and the poet's reflective distance from the world were the defining characteristics of modern writing. He saw Goethe as an exception, a fortunate throwback to earlier simplicity. Yet a poem of Goethe's he could not have known, addressed to Charlotte in the first year of their acquaintance and never published in their lifetimes, tells a different story. It imagines they can now know each other so deeply because they were brother and sister or man and wife in a previous incarnation.[14] Nothing it says about their present life is vivid enough to compete with the imagined past; there is no fulfilled present, the brightest day seems mere twilight, there is only yearning for a life that would match the happiness evoked in the lyrical flashback. One unreality demands another.

There are still traces of this emotional mode in Goethe's travel diary, which pays daily dues to a distant love and on occasion lets fall the word 'yearning'. Yet what he is writing to Charlotte *about* is the Italian reality that now occupies his mind. She is thus ironically the muse of the literary process by which he is fast leaving her world behind—or more precisely, pushing her out of his. The strong presences of Italy and Antiquity leave less and less room for wistfulness

---

[13] Letter 9 in this volume.

[14] 'Warum gabst du uns die tiefen Blicke?' (Why did you [fate] give us such deep insight?), dated 14 Apr. 1776. It was not published until 1848, in Goethe's letters to Charlotte.

and yearning, for harkings-back and distant imaginings, for the old spiritual relationship.

With Christiane, in contrast, Goethe was now engaged in a love affair so solidly present, so free from indirection, inhibition, spiritual complexities, and social conventions and pretensions that it might not have inspired poetry at all, at least on traditional expectations. European love lyric since the Middle Ages had depended on an either/or: either you were happy or you wrote poems. Fulfilled love did not need expression, and as a subject it was too straightforward to yield much poetic substance. But unhappy love gave the poet all the outward causes and inner torments of non-fulfilment to elaborate on. There were exceptions to this pattern, like the fulfilled sensuous poetry of John Donne, but not many. Goethe added another in 1788 with his *Roman Elegies*. They combine the experiences of love and of Italy—whether there was already a love-affair *in* Italy remains a matter of conjecture.[15] More importantly, the cycle combines the two principles Goethe had learned in Italy, solidity and silence: the solidity of real forms, and silence about the 'unreal' emotions for which there was no room in happy love. (There is nothing 'elegiac' about these poems; the title refers only to the verse-form Goethe borrowed from Latin lyric.) Even the lonely newcomer to Rome in Elegy I[16] is not wistfully sighing 'if only', he is eagerly asking 'where?' and 'who?'—asking the buildings around him ('Will you not tell me, stones? O speak, you lofty palazzi') as if he senses a life flowing through the very fabric of the city that he alone is not part of. Once he is, consummation is prompt. By Elegy III he is already reassuring the beloved she is no less respected for yielding so quickly, in a poem that is a veritable hymn to alacrity. The simplicity of its syntax positively squeezes out time—the time of lovers' wishing, waiting, yearning—by appeal to the 'heroic age' of legendary fulfilment between gods and humankind, when 'glances gave rise to desire, what was desired was enjoyed'. Obstacles to love are only practical (a traditional watchful uncle), hurts are curable (a

---

[15] The only piece of halfway solid evidence is Goethe's letter to Carl August of 16 Feb. 1788, which implies in somewhat roundabout phrasing that the Duke had given Goethe advice from his wide experience, and that Goethe has followed it to his benefit. But this is a long way from suggesting an affair, least of all the sort of *love* affair the Elegies describe.

[16] I use the established numbering of the Elegies, not the speculative revision in the Oxford World's Classics volume of Goethe's *Erotic Poems* (see Select Bibliography).

misunderstanding briefly causes jealousy), separation creates not yearning but expectancy. Love is narrated through the concrete objects that are its accomplices and symbols: a table on which an assignation is written in spilled wine; a lamp lit prematurely in the evening to hasten the time when she will be there; a fire that blazes up when she arrives, and which she is skilled at stirring up again from the ashes the morning after. And the wider setting is always the solidity of Rome; the opening appeal to its buildings was not mere rhetoric, they fill the gap left by excluded yearning and frustration. On occasion quite literally: the lover is helped through a particularly long wait by musing on the sights of the city, the physical embodiment of its history. Solidity leaves no space for pining. As the original Latin title *Erotica Romana* made plain, the two elements—Roma and its palindrome Amor—are equally real and equally seriously meant. So is the reciprocity between the stone forms of statues and the live forms of the body; seeing the one and caressing the other heightens the pleasure of both. The lover and art-lover 'sees with an eye that can feel, feels with a hand that can see' (Elegy V).

The *Roman Elegies* are in every sense the most immediate literary product of the Italian journey: they are the first new work Goethe wrote after it, the most direct reference to it, the closest in form and ethos to ancient poetry (the Latin love poets Catullus, Tibullus, Propertius), and for their day a scandalously immediate treatment of sexual love. The classical elegiac couplet and the classical hexameter become the staple forms respectively of Goethe's lyrical and narrative poems for the next decade. Stylistically the new solidity shows up in the reworked and completed novel *Wilhelm Meister's Apprenticeship* in a shift towards more impersonal, objective sentence structures.[17] Systematically in a different way, the scientific views that were confirmed and matured in Italy give Goethe an objective language in which to experiment with the chemistry of human emotions in the later novel *Elective Affinities*. It is always possible, of course, to hear individual echoes of Italy too. When Faust mixes with the crowds outside town on the first day of spring, and declares 'Here nothing stops me being human',[18]

---

[17] See Jane K. Brown, 'The Renaissance of Goethe's Poetic Genius in Italy', in Gerhart Hoffmeister (ed.), *Goethe in Italy, 1786–1986* (Amsterdam, 1988).

[18] *Faust, Part I*, 'Outside the Town Gate', l. 940.

he is catching the mood of Goethe among the Italian populace. But for the most part the effects of Italy are deep in the aesthetic foundations rather than visible on the surface. It may be a matter as much of what is *not* there, of hearing the new silence—in Sherlock Holmes's paradox, of noticing the dog that did not bark. A classical style, that is, may be partly composed of abstentions, as Goethe hinted:

> Every other master we know by the things that he shows us,
> Only the master of style rather by what he withholds.

The implication is that things will be left more and more to speak for themselves. In the plastic arts, Goethe wrote in a letter soon after his return, even the material being worked is part of that process and of the final shape which results; and although literature 'works materials' in a very different sense, the fundamental point holds for his poetics too:

If I were inclined to put something on paper, it would for the present be very simple things. For example, to what extent the material from which a thing has been made influenced the perceptive artist to shape it in this and not some other way. Thus the various kinds of stone allow some very nice conclusions about architecture, every change in the material and the mechanical means determines and constrains the work of art in another way. Here too the ancients were shrewd beyond words. . . . You see that I begin very much from the earth, and it might seem to many people as if I treat the most spiritual matter in too earthly a manner; but I would point out that the gods of the Greeks were enthroned not in a seventh or tenth heaven, but on Olympus and took their giant strides not from one sun to another, but at most from mountaintop to mountaintop[19]

But behind and conditioning all this there is a psychological effect, on both writer and reader. The Italian journey gave Goethe back the creative confidence of his first phase, which had been diverted or eroded by a decade in Weimar. The activities and acquired knowledge of those sober years had now fused into a coherent view—of nature, mankind, society, art—which, for all the objectivity of his aesthetics, was touched once again with excitement. Indeed objectivity and excitement were not a contradiction—that was Goethe's fundamental insight. He now knew in the most all-embracing sense where he stood, and could savour that knowledge.

---

[19] Letter to Christian Gottlieb Heyne, 24 July 1788.

He knew the truth, or at least he felt he did. 'If I know my relation to myself and to the external world, then I call that truth,' he wrote later.[20] The subjective conviction might not have been epistemology enough to satisfy a critical philosopher. Yet Goethe's insistence on earthly realities, his critique of the arbitrary imagination, and his commitment to building afresh on the cleared ground offer a striking parallel, precisely, to Kant's account of the mental faculties in the *Critique of Pure Reason*, published just five years before the poet's Italian journey.

Above all, subjective conviction was enough for the creative writer. It meant a new trust in his perceptions and emotions and in his power to convey them; and in ways that are easier to sense than to analyse, the writer's confidence communicates itself to the reader at every level, from conception and theme down to the nuances of image and tone, so that we feel we too are seeing the world aright through Goethe's eyes. That is the reciprocal confidence that guarantees the poetic currency.

[20] *Maximen und Reflexionen (Maxims and Reflections)*, ed. Max Hecker, no. 198.

NOTE ON THE TEXT AND TRANSLATION

GOETHE's original is preserved in the Goethe-Schiller-Archiv in Weimar and was first published in *Tagebücher und Briefe Goethes aus Italien an Frau von Stein und Herder*, ed. Erich Schmidt, Schriften der Goethe-Gesellschaft 2 (Weimar, 1886). The text is unproblematic, and has been followed in all subsequent printings, including the volume imminent at the time of writing from the Stiftung deutscher Klassik in Weimar, in its complete edition of Goethe's diaries edited by Jochen Goltz, Wolfgang Albrecht, and Andreas Döhler (Stuttgart: Metzler Verlag). Meantime there is the edition *Tagebuch der Italienischen Reise*, ed. Konrad Scheurmann and Jochen Goltz: vol. 1, facsimile; vol. 2, transcription with foreword (Mainz: Philipp von Zabern, 1997). Anyone working on the Italian diary is indebted most of all to Christoph Michel's paperback edition (Frankfurt am Main: Insel, 1976 and reprints), which has scholarship in depth on every aspect of the journey and of Goethe's life at the time. The commentary in vol. 14 of the Berlin edition of Goethe's works, edited by Hans-Heinrich Reuter (Berlin: Aufbau, 1961), and the edition by Horst Rüdiger, *Römische Elegien, Venezianische Epigramme, Tagebuch der Italienischen Reise* (Reinbek: Rowohlt, 1961) provided useful further points.

To keep the personal and period flavour of the Diary, I have retained Goethe's spelling of place-names, which is not always the modern form nor even consistent from one page to another; but his abbreviations have been resolved—'Carlsb.' into 'Carlsbad', etc. Discrepancies between Goethe's text and his tables of arrival and departure times have not been corrected. His mildly inaccurate French and Italian have similarly been left uncorrected. No attempt has been made to translate money values, the implication being clear from context—for example, that fruit is dear in Germany but cheap in Italy, or that the Emperor is getting a tidy sum for the trout-fishing rights at Torbole.

The selection from the letters is designed to take up the story of Goethe's Italian experience from his arrival in Rome onwards, to illustrate the wide range of his interests, and to show his continuing involvement with affairs back in Weimar.

SELECT BIBLIOGRAPHY

Related Works of Goethe

Italian Journey, translated by W. H. Auden and Elizabeth Mayer (1962; Penguin Classics, 1970 and reprints). The work that the older Goethe composed from his documents of the time.

Erotic Poems, translated by David Luke with an introduction by Hans-Rudolf Vaget (Oxford World's Classics, 1997). Contains the *Roman Elegies* (see Introduction, pp. xxii–xxiii) and very properly includes the four elegies suppressed as improper in Goethe's lifetime and long afterwards, though the theory of where they would have fitted into the cycle is speculative and the renumbering unhelpful.

Selected Poems, translated by John Whaley with an introduction by Matthew Bell (Dent, 1998), gives a sense of the full range and power of Goethe's poetry.

Faust Part I, translated by David Luke (Oxford World's Classics, 1987).

Faust Part II, by the same translator (Oxford World's Classics, 1994).

Elective Affinities, translated by David Constantine (Oxford World's Classics, 1994).

Personal, Social, and Cultural Background

Effi Biedrzynski, *Goethes Weimar* (Zurich: Artemis/Winkler, 1992): organized as a reference work but can be read as a series of elegant miniature essays on Weimar personalities, places, and institutions.

W. H. Bruford, *Culture and Society in Classical Weimar 1775–1806* (Cambridge University Press, 1962): offers a rich picture of the people, ideas, and social institutions Goethe interacted with.

Biography and Literary History

George Henry Lewes, *Life and Works of Goethe* (1855): the earliest biography of Goethe in any language and still eminently readable.

Nicholas Boyle, *Goethe. The Poet and the Age*, vol. 1, *The Poetry of Desire* (Oxford University Press, 1991): literary biography of the highest order.

Barker Fairley, *A Study of Goethe* (Oxford University Press, 1947): remains one of the most coherent and persuasive accounts of how the poet's intellectual and emotional life unfolded and shaped his work.

T. J. Reed, *Goethe* (Oxford Past Masters, 2nd edn. 1998): a concise introduction to all aspects of Goethe's work.

T. J. Reed, *The Classical Centre: Goethe and Weimar 1775–1832* (Oxford University Press, 2nd edn. 1986): sets the genesis and achievements of the 'high classical' period in their contemporary context and takes the literary story on to Goethe's death.

John R. Williams, *The Life of Goethe: A Critical Biography* (Blackwells, 1998): a clear, compact account of both life and works.

Aspects of the Italian Experience

James S. Ackermann, *Palladio* (Penguin, 1966): a lucid introduction to the architect who was Goethe's first great aesthetic experience in Italy, which ends (p. 185) with the assessment that 'the only understanding and sympathetic judge of that age was one in whom supreme powers of intellect and of the senses were combined: Goethe'.

Jeffrey Morrison, *Winckelmann and the Notion of Aesthetic Education* (Oxford University Press, 1996): analyses the aesthetics of Italy as Goethe's predecessors had shaped it.

Günter E. Grimm, Ursula Breymeyer, and Walter Erhart (eds.), *'Ein Gefühl von freierem Leben': Deutsche Dichter in Italien* (Stuttgart: Metzler, 1990): a readable survey of German writers' travels in Italy from the seventeenth to the twentieth century.

Konrad Scheurmann and Ursula Bongaerts-Schomer (eds.), *'. . . endlich in dieser Hauptstadt der Welt angelangt!' Goethe in Rom*, 2 vols. (Mainz: Philipp von Zabern, 1997): published to mark the opening of the renovated Casa di Goethe in Rome, comprises a set of essays and a catalogue of the standing exhibition in the house.

Fictions

Peter Hacks, *Ein Gespräch im Hause von Stein über den abwesenden Herrn von Goethe* (A conversation in the von Stein household about the absent Herr von Goethe) (Berlin: Aufbau 1974): imagines Charlotte von Stein's view of the escaped G. and their past relations. The play is not in fact a 'conversation', but a five-act monologue addressed by Charlotte to a (literally) stuffed-shirt husband Josias—a virtuoso piece for solo actress. The letters of her own that Charlotte quotes in Act I are good enough to be true.

Hanns Josef Ortheil, *Faustinas Küsse* (Faustina's Kisses) (Munich: Luchterhand 1988): reconstructs G.'s stay in Rome, with the putative love-affair at the centre of the narrative.

A CHRONOLOGY OF
JOHANN WOLFGANG GOETHE

1749   28 August, Goethe born into a well-to-do family in Frankfurt am Main.

1755   Lisbon Earthquake.

1756–63 Seven Years War.

1752–65 Goethe privately educated. He has tutors in French, Hebrew, Italian, English. His early reading: Klopstock, Homer in translation, the Bible, French classical dramatists.

1765–8 At the University of Leipzig reading Law and a good deal else. Friendships and love affairs (Käthchen Schönkopf), many poems in Rococo style, first comedies. First readings of Shakespeare.

1768   8 June, Winckelmann murdered in Trieste. August 1768–March 1770, Goethe mostly at home in Frankfurt, often ill. Interest in alchemy, association with Pietists.

1770–1 Student in Strasburg, in love with Friederike Brion, friendship with Herder, reading Shakespeare, Ossian, Homer. The breakthrough into his own poetic voice.

1771–4 In Frankfurt and Wetzlar. The first version of *Götz*, in six weeks. Some legal, more literary activity. He writes many of the great poems of his *Sturm und Drang*. First version of *Werther* in the spring of 1774. *Götz* staged in Berlin. Vast success of *Werther*. At some point in these years, begins working on *Faust*.

1775   In love with Lili Schönemann, engagement to her. Journey to Switzerland. *Egmont* begun. Invited to Weimar. Breaks off his engagement. November, arrives in Weimar and is captivated by Charlotte von Stein.

1776   Herder moves to Weimar. Goethe becomes a servant of the State. Goethe's responsibilities—for roads and mines—and his inspection of the Duke's forests generate interests in geology and botany. Also works on anatomy.

1776–86 Ennobled ('von Goethe') in 1782. Growing burden of work for the Weimar Duchy. Writes some poems, but cannot progress with larger projects like *Faust* and *Wilhelm Meister*. Increasing frustration.

1786   September, flight to Italy. Arrives in Rome, 29 October.

1786–8 In Italy: Rome, Naples, Sicily, Rome. Lives among artists, studies intensively to become one and to grasp the nature of ancient art and architecture. *Iphigenie* recast in verse. *Egmont* finished. Further work on *Tasso* and *Faust*.

1788   18 June, back in Weimar. Released from most of his state duties. 12 July, takes Christiane Vulpius as resident mistress. September, the first of the *Roman Elegies*, work on *Tasso*.

1789   French Revolution. *Tasso* completed. 25 December, birth of a son, August, their only child to survive.

1790   March–June, second Italian journey (Venice)—a disappointment.

1792   Goethe in France, at the Battle of Valmy, with the Prussian forces.

1793   21 January, execution of Louis XVI. May–July, Goethe at the Siege of Mainz.

1794   Begins a friendship and literary partnership with Schiller.

1795   *Roman Elegies* published. They give offence.

1796   *Hermann und Dorothea, Wilhelm Meister's Apprenticeship*.

1797   Ballads, with Schiller. In Switzerland again.

1798–9 Poems in classical metres, including a fragmentary continuation of Homer, *Achilleis*. Renewed work on *Faust*.

1799   Schiller moves to Weimar.

1800–5 Poems, work on *Faust*, a great deal of scientific work.

1805   Death of Schiller. Goethe ill, withdrawn, depressed.

1806   *Faust, Part I* completed. Prussians defeated by Napoleon at Jena. Goethe marries Christiane Vulpius.

1807–9 Relationship with Minna Herzlieb. *Elective Affinities*, work on *Wilhelm Meister's Years of Travel*. Begins work on the autobiography *Poetry and Truth*. Received by Napoleon, awarded the Cross of the Legion of Honour.

1812   Goethe meets Beethoven. The French retreat from Moscow.

1815   Waterloo.

1814–18 Relationship with Marianne von Willemer. Writes the cycle of 'Persian' poems, the *West-Östlicher Divan*.

1816   6 June, death of Christiane.

1816–17 Publication of *Italian Journey*.

1821   First version of *Wilhelm Meister's Years of Travel*.

1823–4 In love with Ulrike von Levetzow, writes the three poems of the *Trilogie der Leidenschaft*. From 1823, conversations with Eckermann.

1825–31 Work on *Faust, Part II*, completed shortly before Goethe's death.

1829 Final version of *Wilhelm Meister's Years of Travel*.

1832 Dies, 22 March.

MAPS

Goethe's routes to Rome 1786, to Naples and Sicily 1787 and return to Germany 1788.

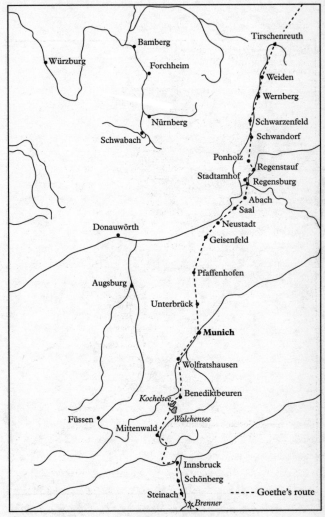

Goethe's route to the Brenner Pass, September 1786

THE FLIGHT TO ITALY

The Diary of the Poet's Journey in September and October 1786

FIRST SECTION
FROM CARLSBAD TO THE BRENNER PASS
1786

Stations from Carlsbad to the Brenner Pass in the Tyrol
covered between 3 and 8 September 1786

Name	Distance (Stages)		Arrived	Departed
		3rd		
Tzwoda	$1\frac{1}{2}$		$\frac{1}{2}$ past 7 a.m.	soon after
Eger	$1\frac{1}{2}$		12 noon	2
Tischenreuth	$1\frac{1}{2}$		5	straight away
Weyden	2		9	straight away
		4th		
Wernberg	1		1	—
Schwarzenfeld	$1\frac{1}{4}$		$2\frac{1}{2}$	—
Schwandorf	1		$4\frac{1}{2}$	—
Bahnholz	$1\frac{1}{4}$		$7\frac{1}{2}$	—
Regenspurg	$1\frac{1}{4}$		10	
		5th		$12\frac{1}{2}$ noon
Saal	$1\frac{1}{2}$		3	$3\frac{1}{2}$
Neustadt	$1\frac{1}{2}$		6	straight away
Geisenfeld	$1\frac{1}{2}$		8	—
Pfaffenhofen	$1\frac{1}{2}$		10	—
Unterbrück	$1\frac{1}{2}$	6th	2	—
Munich	2		6 a.m.	
	$21\frac{3}{4}$			
		7th		
Wohlfahrtshausen	2		9 a.m.	soon after
Benedicktbayern	2		$1\frac{1}{2}$	straight away
Wallensee	$1\frac{1}{2}$		$4\frac{1}{2}$	straight away
Mittelwald	$1\frac{1}{2}$		$7\frac{1}{2}$	

Name	Distance (Stages)	Arrived	Departed
		8th	6 a.m.
Seefeld	1	8½	
Innsbruck	1½	11	2
Schemberg	1	4	
Steinach	1	5½	
Brenner	1	7½ p.m.	
	12½	9th	7 p.m.
from p. 1	21¾		
	34¼		

On 3 September at 3 in the morning I crept out of Carlsbad, they wouldn't have let me go if I hadn't. They could tell I wanted to get away. Countess Lanthieri* dropped a dreadfully heavy hint, but I wasn't going to be stopped, for it was time. I was already keen to go on the 28th. But that was no good, I still had too many things to settle.

At half-past 7 in Zwota, lovely calm misty morning. In Eger by 12, the sunshine hot. The morning had been overcast, the high clouds fluffy strips, the lower ones heavy, the weather holding steady, wind south-west. Thoughts about this. The weather was already auspicious on the 2nd. More of this in Supplement a.*

I discovered that Eger was on the same latitude as Frankfurt, and felt happy to be eating my lunch almost on the 50th parallel again. From Carlsbad to Zwota, quartzy sandstone; the road to Maria Culm goes over mountain terrain of sedimentary rock. Arable plain as far as Eger.

In Bavaria the first thing you come upon is the monastery of Waldsassen, a valuable possession of people who were shrewd enough to get in before others. It lies in a fertile shallow depression, not to say a basin, the valley bottom fine meadowland, surrounded on all sides by gentle fertile slopes, and they own property far and wide in the area. The soil is a weathered mix of clay and slate loosened by the quartz that was in it and isn't itself dissolved. The position still elevated, but charming, the fields fertile.

As far as Tischenreuth the land rises, the streams flow towards you on their way down to the Eger and the Elbe; from Tischenreuth onwards, the land falls away southward and the streams flow towards the Danube.

Tischengreut by five. Excellent road surface of granite sand, you couldn't imagine a more perfect. The region it goes through all the worse, granite sand too, low-lying, boggy and so on. As you're now on good road and going downhill, you get on incredibly fast, a real contrast to the snail's pace of Bohemian roads. I was in Weyda by half-past eight, 1 in the morning at Wernberg, half-past two Schwarzenfeld, half-past four Schwandorf, half-past seven Bahn-holtz, at ten Regensburg—and so I'd done these $12\frac{1}{4}$ stages or about 113 miles* in 31 hours.

On the way from Schwandorf to Regenstauff, as day was starting to break, I noticed the soil changing for the better. Tidal movement from the Danube in ancient times had operated all the way up the River Regen to form natural polders, which we now make use of. You see this in the vicinity of all big rivers. I think I've talked about it before. Regenspurg is very beautiful, the spot had to attract a town. And the clerical gentlemen got a good hold on things; all the fields around the town belong to them, and within its walls there are churches and monasteries at every turn.

The Danube reminded me of the old Main. The river and bridge at Frankfurt make a finer show, but here the town of Stadt am Hof on the far bank is a delightful picture.

The Jesuit school was giving its annual performance today, I went straight in, saw the start of the tragedy and the end of the opera. They did it no worse than a young amateur company. And the costumes were very fine, almost too splendid. This too, and the whole set-up, which I'll tell you about some time, convinced me once again of the Jesuits' immense shrewdness; and it isn't the kind of abstract shrewdness we tend to think, they also take a pleasure in what they do, they enjoy it and enjoy themselves, it comes from an involvement in real life. How glad I am that I'm advancing deep into the Catholic heartland and getting to know it in its full scope.

If only you were with me, I'd be talkative all day, for the constant flow of new objects gives rise to a hundred observations. I often wish I had Fritz* with me, and I'm alone and stay alone.

It's impossible to express how happy my way of seeing the world makes me, and what I'm learning every day! and how, really, there's scarcely any existence that is a mystery for me. Everything simply speaks to me and shows me its nature. And as I don't have a servant, I'm friends with the whole world. Any beggar will tell me the way— and I talk to the people I meet as if we were old acquaintances. I'm really enjoying it.

Today I'm writing to you precisely on the 49th parallel and it's made a promising start, the morning was cool and people are complaining how cold and wet it is here as well, but it turned out a magnificent mild day, and the air that a great river carries with it is something quite different.

The fruit here is nothing special, still I live in hopes that it soon will be. I bought a penn'orth of pears from an old woman I met down by the water and ate them for all to see like any other schoolboy. God grant me grapes and figs soon. I'll enclose a layout of Regensburg, and the Jesuit play.

NB Jesuit churches, towers, decoration generally! Something great in the conception that secretly instils reverence in all men. Gold, silver, metals and magnificence, riches to dazzle beggars of all classes, and here and there something tasteless so that humanity is reconciled and attracted. This is the genius of Catholic outward piety in general, but I've never yet seen it carried through with so much understanding, skill, taste, and consistency as in the Jesuits, and all their churches have a common style. More about this later. How they haven't continued the old deadened devotion of the other religious orders but have moved with the spirit of the times.

Regensburg 5 September

From Carlsbad I'd brought no more than a saddlebag and rucksack, and that would be room and to spare for my clothes, but as I have so many books and papers with me it was all too much. Now I've bought myself a small case which is just right. It's also a very good thing that I'm by myself, for I'm sure being waited on hand and foot makes you old and incapable before your time. Now everything gives me more pleasure, and it's as if I'm beginning again at the beginning.

I certainly hope to get rid of a few big failings that I've picked up.
Drew by the Danube.

half-past eleven

I must get away from this place! An assistant in Montag's bookshop who used to work at Hofmann's recognized me. So there you are, authors can't expect any good from booksellers! But I looked him straight in the eye and quite calmly denied it was me.

I've seen Pastor Schäfer and his collections, I went under the name Möller, which I shall keep to. Farewell for now, it's on to Munich.

There's a strange kind of rock here made into quarrystones, a sort of conglomerate, but of something I think is older and original. It's greenish, mixed with quartz, full of holes, and with large pieces of finest jasper in it, in which in turn there are small round flakes of the conglomerate. One specimen was really too tempting, but the stone was stuck too fast, and I've sworn not to load myself with stones on this journey.

the 5th, left Regensburg half-past midday.

Lovely stretch around Aburg where the Danube breaks against limestone cliffs, nearly as far as Saale.

It's the same sort of limestone as at Osterode in the Harz Mountains. Dense, but full of holes.

3 o'clock in Saale.

Left Saale at half-past 3, in Neustadt by six, Geisenfeld by eight, Pfaffenhofen by 10, Unterbrück at 2 in the morning of the 6th, Munich by 6 o'clock.

Six o'clock in the evening. Well, I've done the rounds of Munich, I'll sleep here tonight and go on tomorrow. You see, I'm adapting pretty quickly, and I simply must and will try this way of doing things to get out of my old dragging inertia.

I've seen the picture gallery and got my eyes used to pictures again. There are some outstanding things here. Rubens's* sketches for the Luxembourg are splendid. Another thing they have here is that noble plaything, a model of Trajan's column, the figures gilt silver on lapis lazuli (I think Archenholz* has a description of it). It really is a fine piece of work.

In the Antiquarium or cabinet of antiquities I saw that my eyes just weren't adjusted to these objects, and I didn't want to linger and waste time. There's a lot that I just can't get on with.

I was struck by a Drusus, I liked the two Antonines, and a few other things besides. The exhibits are not well displayed either, although plainly the intention is to impress, and the room, it's more like a vaulted hall, would look good if they only kept it better and cleaner.

In the natural history section, I found some fine items from the Tyrol, but they were things I already knew through Knebel.* Talking of Knebel! When he saw the antiquities here, he greatly liked a Julius Caesar which (unless I'm terribly mistaken) is quite worthless, but it does have a striking resemblance to Knebel himself. It seems the correspondence of character made up for the lack of art.

I'm staying at Knebel's old inn too, but don't want to ask them about him for fear of arousing suspicion, or confirming it. Nobody here's recognized me, and I enjoy going about among them like that. I paid a call on Kobel,* but he wasn't at home. For the rest, I had the fun of seeing a few people I knew by name and observing their behaviour.

Altogether, now I know how the different classes feel and since nobody can conceal their status, or wants to, I have a great advantage, even without my physiognomic knowledge,* and it's incredible how human characteristics stand out.

Herder* is probably right that I'm still just a big child, and it's nice that I can go on in my childish way now as much as I like.

Tomorrow it's straight on to Innsbruck! I'm leaving out Salzburg, which I'd have loved to tell you about to outdo that French traveller,* the Ziller valley with its tourmalines, the mines at Schwaz, the salt-works at Halle! The things I'm leaving out, so as to carry through the one idea that has almost grown too old in my soul.

Today I found a woman selling figs in one of the castle galleries, I promptly bought some and though they were dear and three kreuzers each, still they were the first, with more to follow, God willing. The fruit isn't that special for the 48th parallel. People complain as everywhere about the cold and the wet. A mist, or perhaps it was more like rain, greeted me this morning just before Munich, all day there was a cold wind coming down from the Austrian Alps, the sky was overcast. I climbed the tower that young woman threw herself off,* and tried to see the mountains of the Tyrol. But they were covered in mist and the whole sky clouded over. Now there's evening sunshine still just catching the old tower outside my window. Farewell. I think of you all the time, and I often find myself wishing I'd brought Fritz with me.

Another tricky job I've got to do. After a final consultation with

Herder, I had to bring Iphigenie* with me and now I've got to go through the text some time and spend at least a few days on it. I will too, as soon as I've found some small place that I fancy staying at.

7 September, evening. It seems my guardian spirit is saying amen to my creed, and I'm thankful to him, not for making this splendid day for me, but because this was the day on which he brought me here. As I was getting off, the coachman said it was the first day like it this whole summer. I feel a deep, calm, thankful joy at my good fortune, and trust it will now go on like this.

It was 5 o'clock when I left Munich. Clear sky. Clouds were settled over the mountains of the Tyrol, and the strips of cloud lower down weren't moving either. The way goes along the Isar, up above it on alluvial hills of gravel, the work of old high waters. The mists on the river and water-meadows held out for a while, in the end they were burned off too.

In between the gravel hills just mentioned (which you have to imagine going on for several hours in all directions) there is the finest fertile soil. Just before Wohlfahrtshausen, which I got to at 9 o'clock and thus reached the 48th parallel, you have to rejoin the Isar, there's a cut and a gravel slope, about 150 feet high. In Wohlfahrtshausen the sun was positively burning. Everyone was complaining about the bad weather and that the *good Lord* won't do a thing about it. Now the new world started to open up for me, I was getting close to the mountains, they were coming out of the clouds. Benedict Bayern is a delightful sight! When you first see it, it lies in a fertile plain, a long and broad white building and a broad and high mountain ridge behind it. Then you come down to the Cochelsee, then to the Walchersee. Seeing the first snow-covered peak, I wanted to wave my hat, yet I still couldn't grasp the fact that I was already so close to the snowy mountains. Then I heard it had rained and thundered and lightened in these parts yesterday and snowed on the tops. So what I was saluting was the season's first snow.

The high cliffs are of limestone, the oldest kind that doesn't yet have fossils in. These limestone rocks run in an immense uninterrupted sequence from Dalmatia all the way to the Gotthard and even farther. Haquet* travelled a great part of the chain. More of that another time. They are in contact with granite, porphyry, etc. I only found a few pieces, a kind of gneiss, in mountain stream beds.

Wallensee by half-past four. After which I hadn't gone far when I

had my first small adventure. A harpist was walking in front of us
with his daughter, a girl of 11, and he asked me to give her a lift. I let
her get in beside me and took her as far as the next village. A well-
behaved and well-trained little thing that had seen a good deal of the
world, made the pilgrimage to Maria Einsiedeln with her mother,
and always travelled on foot. In Munich she'd played before the
Elector and had already been heard by 21 princely personages all
told. She kept me well entertained, had handsome big brown eyes
and a wayward forehead that she raised slightly. Was pretty and
natural when she talked, especially when she laughed out loud in her
childish way. She tried to make her silences meaningful too and
would purse her upper lip and put on a dark expression. I chatted to
her about all sorts of things. She was at home everywhere, and very
observant. Once she asked me what kind of tree that was. It was a
maple, and the first I'd seen on the whole journey. She'd spotted it
straight away. There were more further on. She showed me a new
bonnet she'd had made in Munich and was carrying in a hatbox.

The weather was going to be good at least for a few days, she said.
They carried their barometer with them, which was their harp; if the
strings went sharp it meant fair weather, and today they had. I
accepted the omen and had a lot more amusing talk with her until we
parted. Arrived Mittelwald half-past 7.

8 September. Evening
Reached the Brenner, virtually forced to stop at what is an ideal place
for a rest. My first act is to tell you all the good things of the day just
past. It was the kind of day you can savour in the memory for years.

Left Mittelwald at 6, clear sky, a keen wind blowing, and the kind
of cold only allowed in February. The near slopes dark and covered
in spruce, the grey limestone cliffs, the highest white peaks against
the beautiful blue of the sky made exquisite, constantly changing
pictures.

Near Scharnitz you get into the Tyrol and the border is closed
with a rampart that seals off the valley and joins up with the mountains. It looks very fine. On one side the cliff is fortified, on the other
it just goes steeply up.

At Seefeld by half-past 8.

From there the route gets steadily more interesting. Up to this
point it went over the hills that you climb out of Benedict Bayern,

now you get nearer to the valley of the Inn and look down into Intzingen. The sun was high and hot. The clothes I brought with me—a jerkin with sleeves and an overcoat—that were meant for all seasons, had to be changed, and they often are 10 times in a day.

Near Cirl the route drops into the Inn valley. The situation is indescribably lovely and with the heat-haze high up it was magnificent. I only managed to dash down a sketch, the driver hadn't been to Mass yet and was in a hurry to get to Inspruck, it was the Nativity of the Virgin.

Now it's down the Inn valley all the way, past the immense steep limestone face of the Martin Wall. At the point where Emperor Max is said to have got himself cragfast,* I reckon I could probably get up and down without an angel's help, though it would still be a criminally risky undertaking.

Innspruck lies in a splendid position, in a broad rich valley between high rock walls and mountains.

I felt like stopping there for today, but something inside wouldn't let me rest.

The innkeeper's son was Söller to a T.* So I'm gradually coming across the characters I've invented.

It's the Virgin's Nativity. The people are all dressed up, looking healthy and prosperous, and making a pilgrimage to Wilten a quarter of an hour outside town. I left Innsbruck at 2 and at half-past seven was here

on the Brenner.

Here's where I'm going to rest up, and here I'll review the last six days for you and then travel on.

The way up from Innspruck gets more and more beautiful, it's no good trying to describe it. You come up a ravine down which the water plunges to the Inn. A ravine that has countless variations.

At some points the side opposite you isn't so steep that they can't grow the finest crops. There are small settlements, houses, chalets, churches, all painted white, between fields and hedges on the high, sloping ground.

At other points it gets narrower, there's just pasture, the valley falls steeply away etc.

I've acquired a good deal for my 'Creation'.* Yet nothing wholly new or unexpected. Also I've kept dreaming of the model* I've been talking about for so long, which would be the only way to give you dear laypeople a clear picture of the thoughts I carry around with me all the time.

Finally it grew dark and darker, the detail of the view was lost, the masses got larger and more splendid. In the end, when everything was shifting before my eyes like a deep mysterious picture, I suddenly saw the high tops picked out in the moonlight again and the stars winking down.

I'd love to spend a month with you in and around Innspruck, I mean in weather like I've had today. And all the way up through the mountains, what subjects I've driven past, which would give you immense pleasure if you could draw them. I'll send you some samples.

Now I'm here, and have got a very clean comfortable guest-house; I'm going to take a rest, think over these past days and put everything in order for you, and prepare myself for the next bit of the journey.

Weather see Supplement a. Latitude, Supplement b. Plants Supplement c. Mountains, rock types, Supplement d. People Supplement e.

9 September, evening
Now that I gather my brief observations of these few days, write them up, and bind them together, it turns out they're almost becoming a book, I dedicate it to you. It may not be much, still, it will give you pleasure and help me later on to put together a more ordered and detailed narrative. We'll enjoy reading about these regions now because I've seen them and thought a bit about them, and you shall enjoy them through me. I'll go on like this taking an occasional rest day and putting what's happened in some kind of order, it's no good just letting things accumulate and in the end one doesn't want to look at the individual pages.

Up here in this well-built, tidy, comfortable house I look back once more in your direction. From here some streams flow towards Germany, some towards Italy, and these I hope to follow tomorrow. How strange to think that twice already I've stood at a similar point, rested, and not got across.* I shan't believe it either till I'm down there. What other people find commonplace and easy, life makes tough going for me. Farewell! Think of me at this crucial moment of my life. I'm well, free of worries, and you'll see from these pages how I'm enjoying the world. Farewell. The whole day's gone by on these papers.

Supplement a
Thoughts about the weather

As soon as I saw the high fleecy cloud back in Carlsbad on the 2nd, I felt hopeful, I concluded: that the atmosphere was regaining its elasticity and in process of restoring the good weather. But I didn't think of what I believe I've noticed since, namely: *that a more elastic atmosphere consumes the clouds, breaks up their coherent mass*, so that the vapours that were formerly pressed together—that moved about as clouds, only drifted at a certain height above the earth, fell as rain, were driven up again as mist—that these vapours are now evenly distributed everywhere. Since contact with atmospheric electricity can make every drop of water or vapour infinitely elastic, or indeed can divide it into infinitely small droplets, so too the total water mass can spread to a far greater height and vanish from our sight, so that finally not the least trace of vapour is visible. Perhaps what I'm saying is already well known, I'm simply putting down my observations and drawing conclusions from my hypothesis.

When an immense quantity of condensed vapours is to be dissolved, as on this occasion, it's a slow process, and the upper atmosphere being first to get back its elasticity is first to begin forming a 'sheep-sky' (small clouds loosely joined to each other like combed wool). In the high mountains, which attract and hold clouds, these start to take firm shape as great towering mountain-like masses, while the clouds of the lower atmosphere drift beneath them as grey strips and in heavy elongated shapes. If the elasticity of the atmosphere goes on increasing, it operates from above to consume the clouds that are gathered round the mountains, and the wind from the mountains which a few days before brought rain now brings good weather.

I quite clearly saw one such cloud consumed, it clung to the mountain, dissolved very very slowly, at most a few wisps could be seen to split off and rise into the air but then immediately disappear. And so the cloud gradually vanished and behind the mountain I noticed in the air very light, small white strips, which I also finally lost sight of altogether.

Now if water is distributed in this way throughout the atmosphere and still to some extent kept together, you can see it quite clearly by the way it affects the view and separates out the different bands of background in the landscape. It has to fall as dew, or hoar-frost, or else expand and spread further. This time the weather around the Tyrolese mountains put a violent end to it with thunder and lightning and snow; then it turned bright again.

In just the same way on the 9th, when the sun was starting to melt the summit snows, I saw light foamy strips rising and spreading in a cold south wind far across the sky northwards. And so it went on, more and more white haze came up from the south, the whole sky became overcast and the sun was eventually obscured, the vapours turned into clouds which still moved at some height, and the local people lamented that there'd soon be more rain.

Further explanation in line with my theory: The atmosphere in this area was now almost saturated with vapour, so could no longer totally consume it, and therefore had to allow the moisture to become a uniform mist and finally grow more compact, turning into clouds. If in the course of the night the cooling process reduces the elasticity of the water and increases the elasticity of the air, so that the latter gets the upper hand, then the clouds are bound to be attracted by the mountains again and to precipitate.

One more observation. The atmosphere and the mountains alternately attract the moisture, under what conditions this happens will be explicable. For the moment just this much: if the elasticity of the air increases, so does its attractive power and the clouds leave the mountains and are borne up and consumed by the air, as I've already said, and vice versa. It's like a hot-air balloon that similarly gains height when the air becomes more elastic.

I've used the word 'elasticity', instead of 'gravity' which is more usual in discussing these things, and it really is better. But in general my technical terms are not the best, when I come back we'll compare my observations and experiences with the principles and experiments of the physicists. Unfortunately I'm not a specialist,* as you know.

Supplement b
Latitude, Climate, etc.

The whole way I've been joking to myself about latitude, climate, and everything connected with it, so here are a few words on that.

It's not latitude that makes the difference, it's the mountain ridges that cut across a country east–west. These at once produce enormous changes and the countries immediately to the north of them have to suffer the consequences. This year's weather for the whole of the north seems to have been determined by the great alpine chain on which I'm writing this. Here they've had rain all summer, and south-west and south-east winds have spread rain from here in the whole of the north. In Italy they've apparently had beautiful weather and almost too dry.

Supplement c
Plants, Fruit, etc.

What I've met with so far in the way of fruit hasn't been up to much. Apples and pears grow in the Inn valley before you reach Inspruck, peaches and grapes they import from Italy or strictly speaking from southern Tyrol. Around Inspruck they cultivate maize, the ears were just setting.

Another plant they call polenta (elsewhere buckwheat) that gives a brownish grain from which they make flour that gets cooked as a mash or as dumplings.

After Innsbruck I saw the first larches, which occur frequently up here, and near Schemberg the first stonepine. On plants I still feel very much a learner.

As far as Munich I only saw the common varieties. *Hieracium* (the blue flower that at home they call wild celery), yarrow, thistles, which I saw constantly all the way from Carlsbad. By a ditch outside Munich the plumed pink, a sort of low-growing sunflower. Coming up into the hills beyond Benedict Bayern and by the Walchsee, there were others that I pressed, and the first gentian; it was always near water that I found the new plants first.

In general on the effect of barometric height on plants, here's an opinion that needs to be tested.

The more elastic air influences the plant's organs so that they expand fully, making its form more perfect. If there is enough moisture present that can penetrate into the expanded organ, the plant is well nourished and can develop to the full, grow stronger and propagate itself more amply. This thought occurred to me looking at a willow and a gentian when I saw that they were very delicate and the nodes were well apart.

Instead of being like fig. 1, they were shaped as in fig. 2.

More of this anon.

NB I also saw very tall rushes in the Walchensee.

Supplement d
Mountains and Rock Specimens

I said before that I've been travelling through the limestone alps. They have a grey look and beautiful strange, irregular forms, although the rock also splits into layers and beds. But as you also get twisted layers and the rock in general weathers unevenly, the peaks have a strange appearance.

It was all limestone as far as I could observe up to here. In the vicinity of the lake the character of the mountains changes (perhaps sooner, that's something for a follow-up study) and I found mica schist strongly cut by veins of quartz. Steel-green and dark grey. Outcropping above it there was a dense white limestone, micacious at the detachments and coming away in great masses which however were endlessly cleft in themselves. On top of the limestone, mica schist outcropped, but this seemed to me more delicate.

Higher up there was a particular kind of gneiss, or rather a granite variety more similar to gneiss, like that piece I have from the Ellenbogen region.

Up here opposite the house the rock is mica schist, and the waters that come off the mountains nearest by carry both it and grey limestone.

So it shows that up here somewhere nearby must be the granite basement it all rests on.

You can see from the map that we're on the flank of the actual great Brenner from which the water flows away all round. Doing the circuit of it would be a good project for a young mineralogist.

Supplement e
People

I can't say much about them except what I've seen of their look. They're a sound and straightforward nation, much of a muchness in build, but I won't venture an impromptu description of their physique.

I particularly noted large brown eyes and very clearly defined eyebrows in the women, and in contrast fair eyebrows and broad in the men. The green hats have a cheery look here among the mountains. They wear them decorated with ribbons or broad scarves of taffeta with fringes, very neatly pinned on, and everybody has a flower or a feather stuck in their hat.

The women on the other hand wear very broad white hats of shaggy cotton, rather like a shapeless men's nightcap, which gives them a really outlandish look.

The rest of their costume is well known.

I've had occasion to notice how much store the ordinary people set by peacock feathers, and how highly all kinds of bright feathers are prized, so I'd advise any traveller who wants to please folk by giving a big tip that won't cost too much to take these kind of feathers with him. It goes without saying that you have to make a tactful job of the giving.

SECOND SECTION
FROM THE BRENNER TO VERONA

Stations from the Brenner Pass in the Tyrol to Verona
covered between 9 and 14 September

Name	Distances (Stages)	Arrived	Departed
	9th		
Sterzingen		9 p.m.	$9\frac{1}{2}$
Mittenwalde	each	12	
Brixen	time	10th $3\frac{1}{2}$	
Colmann	one	5	
Deutschen	stage	7	straight away
Botzen	the	9	
Brandsol	stage	11	
Neumarck	9	$1\frac{1}{2}$	
Salurn	miles	$2\frac{1}{2}$	$3\frac{1}{2}$
Neefes	$1\frac{1}{2}$	6	
Trient	$1\frac{1}{2}$	$7\frac{1}{2}$	5 p.m.
	11th		
Aqua viva	1	$6\frac{1}{2}$	
Roveredo	$1\frac{1}{2}$	$8\frac{1}{2}$	
	12th		
Porto al Lago di Garda properly Torbole.	$2\frac{1}{2}$	8	4 a.m.
	13th		5 a.m.
Malsesine		7	after midnight
	14th		
Bartolino		10	straight away
Verona.		2	

Trent 10 September. 8 p.m.

I've now been alive for fully 50 hours, constantly active and on the move. If I were to let myself go, I'd also tell you what's been happening to me. But if I'm to be fit for tomorrow I'd better have a good night's rest, so you shall hear from me in the morning. Good night for now.

11th, early

My narrative continued.

On the evening of the 9th when I'd concluded my first section for you, I tried to draw the hostelry but it was no good, I got the shapes wrong and went back indoors feeling a bit cross.

The landlord asked whether I wouldn't like to move on, there'd be a moon etc., and though I knew very well he needed the horses early the next morning and wanted them back home by then, so he was really out for his own interests, still I accepted because it fitted my own impulse, the sun shone through again and the air was very agreeable.

I packed my things and left the Brenner at seven. As I'd hoped, the atmosphere got the better of the clouds and it was a really fine evening.

The driver fell asleep and the horses went off downhill on their familiar route at a very smart trot, they slowed up all the more when on the flat stretches, he'd wake up and drive them on, so I got down very speedily between the high cliffs to the torrential River Etsch.* The moon rose and lit up tremendous subjects. Some mills above the stream were pure Everdingens.* If only I could have given your eyes the chance to see them.

At 9 I got to Sterzing and they made it clear they wanted me off again straight away, at 12 in Mittelwald everyone was fast asleep except the coachmen, the same in Brixen at half-past 2, and by daylight I was in Colman. Sorry though I was to race through these interesting regions like a bird of night (the speed they took it at was often hair-raising) still, I rejoiced that it was like a wind behind me blowing me on towards my wishes.

At daybreak I saw the first vineyards, we passed a woman with pears and peaches, and on we went to Deutschen, where I arrived at 7 and at last I saw before me, after actually driving northwards a bit and with the sun now fully up, the valley in which Botzen lies.

Surrounded by steep mountains that are cultivated up to a considerable height, it's open to the south, protected to the north by the Tyrolean ranges, there's a mild, gentle air all round, the Etsch here turns southward. There are vineyards on the foothills. The stems are drawn over long, low trellises and the blue grapes hang richly and very decoratively from the top laths. On the valley bottom too, where further north you'd expect meadows, grapes are grown in similar close-packed rows of trellises, with maize in between, called in Italian *Fromentass* or further on *Fromentone*,[1] which here grows ever higher. I've often seen it up to 9–10 feet. The fibrous male blossom hasn't yet been cut, they do that a little while after pollination.

In hot sun on to Botzen, where everyone makes their living from the fair. Seeing the many merchant faces all together was a delight, their purposeful, contented existence expresses itself very vividly.

There were women selling fruit in the square, from baskets 4 to $4\frac{1}{2}$ feet in section and flat, with the peaches laid out side by side, the pears too. I remembered what I saw in Regensburg written up in the window of an inn:

> Comme les pêches et les melons
> Sont pour la bouche d'un baron
> Ainsi les verges et les bâtons
> Sont pour les fous, dit Salomon.*

It's obvious a baron from up north wrote this, and it's just as natural that he would change his way of thinking if he lived down here.

The Botzen fair has a strong line in silks, other textiles are brought in there and it gathers in any leather goods from the mountains and the country round. It's also the main place where the merchants come to collect their money.

I hurried on in case anyone should recognize me, and in any case there was nothing to keep me there. Though to tell the truth it's the urge and unrest that are driving me; for I would have quite liked to look round a bit and have a chance to see all the products that get brought together here. Still, I console myself with the thought that it must all be in print somewhere. In our statistical times* you don't

---

[1] They pronounce it Formentass, and Formenton is the polenta I mentioned earlier. (G.)

have to worry too much about these things, someone else is bound to have taken the job on, what I'm after now is the sense impressions that no book and no picture can give me, so that I start to take an interest in the world again and try out how observant I can be, and also see how far my studies and acquired knowledge will take me, whether and how far my eye is single, pure, and undimmed,* what I can pick up as I rush by, and whether the creases my mind has got set in can possibly be smoothed out again.

If I make further progress, I'll tell you more.

I already feel that the fact of looking after myself, with no servant, so that I have to keep an eye on my situation all the time, has given me in these last few days a quite new elasticity of mind. I have to watch the exchange rate, change money, pay for things, make notes, write to you, where before I was only ever thinking, deciding, reflecting, commanding, and dictating. From Botzen to Trient[1] (for the stations, see list) the road goes through a more and more fertile valley. Everything that is just beginning to come on further north, down here has more strength and vitality, it makes you believe in a god again.

The Etsch flows more quietly, in many places it forms broad stretches of gravel, on the ground near the river and on the hills the plants all grow so densely intermingled that you'd think they would stifle each other. Vineyards, maize, buckwheat, mulberries, nuts, quinces. The dwarf-elder flings itself vigorously over the walls, the ivy grows in strong stems up the rocks and spreads far beyond them, and the lizards slither away across the stones.

If only I could enjoy this region and this atmosphere with you, you would really feel well here.

Even the casual passers-by recall the most delightful paintings. The women's piled-up plaits, the men's bare chests and light jackets, the splendid oxen they drive home from market, the little asses with their loads, it all makes a living and moving Heinrich Roos.*

And then when it's evening and there are just a few clouds resting on the mountains and barely moving across the sky, and as soon as the sun goes down you hear the crickets start chirping! I feel as if I

---

[1] NB A poor woman who asked me to let her child ride in the coach because the hot ground was burning its feet. Strange get-up the child was wearing. I spoke to her in Italian, whereupon she said she didn't understand German. (G.)

was born and brought up here, and am now coming back from a whaling voyage to Greenland. Everything feels welcome, even the dust of my homeland that sometimes lies thick on the roads and which I've not seen for so long.

The ringing or rather tinkling sound of the grasshoppers is most delightfully penetrating and not at all unpleasant.

It's funny when mischievous lads start whistling in competition with a field of grasshoppers. It sounds like they really get each other going. Today is another marvellous day, particularly a mildness in the air that there's no way I can convey.

If anyone read that who lived in the south, came from the south, he'd think I was childish. Oh the things I'm writing are things I've long known, all the time I was suffering with you under a bad sky, and now I'm glad to feel this happiness as an exception, when we ought to enjoy it all the time as a permanent favour of nature.

The rest, see the appended supplements, which for convenience sake I will continue with the same letter designations as in the first Section.

Trient. I've been walking around in the town, which is very ancient, and in some of its streets has new, well-built houses. There's a picture in the church of the whole assembled Council* listening to a sermon by the Jesuit General. I'd like to know what he's telling them.

I went into the Jesuit church, which is distinguished by the red pilasters outside, there's a big curtain just inside the door to keep the dust out, an iron grille closes off the church from a small antechapel, so that you can see everything but not get in. All was quiet and as if dead, the door was only open because at vespers all the churches are. As I'm just standing there and thinking about the style of the building, which I found similar to the well-known churches, along comes an old man wearing a black biretta, which he at once takes off, and a long black coat turned grey with age, kneels down in front of the grille, and after a short prayer gets up again. As he turns to go, he says half to himself: well, now they've driven the Jesuits out, they should have paid them what the church cost, I know very well what it cost, and how many thousands for the seminary (by this time he was outside the curtain again, I stepped up to the curtain, looked out at the side, and kept quiet, he'd stopped on the threshold) it wasn't the Emperor did it, it was the Pope, he continued with his face to the street and without suspecting I was there. First the Spaniards, then the French (he named a few others); Abel's blood cries out against his brother Cain!—and off he went, all the time talking to himself, down the steps and away down the street.

I suspect that he was either a Jesuit himself or somebody they looked after, and perhaps he had lost his reason over the tremendous collapse of the Order,* and now he comes to the empty receptacle looking for its old inmates, says a brief prayer, and pronounces a curse on their enemies.

My companion* pointed out to me in some wonderment a house they call the Devil's House, for which it is said not only were the stones brought to the spot but the whole thing was built in a single night. The most devilish thing about it, though, was something he didn't notice, which is that it's the only house of any taste that I saw in Trient. It dates back to an early period but was certainly the work of a good Italian architect.

5 p.m. on to Roveredo.

The same views as yesterday evening and the grasshoppers that start their shrill song as soon as the sun sets. For about 5 miles beyond the town you are travelling between walls over which you can see the vine-frames, other walls that aren't high enough have been raised with stones, brushwood, and other ingenious means to prevent passers-by plucking the grapes, many owners spray the ones nearest the road with lime, which makes them unpalatable and is bad for the stomach but doesn't do the wine any harm because it must come out in the fermentation. The fine weather is continuing. It was very hot about 3 o'clock when I took a walk out of the town and on to the bridge. I feel like a child that still has to learn to live again. Nobody here shuts their doors, the windows are left open all the time, etc. Nobody wears boots, there's not a cloth coat to be seen. I'm a real northern bear down from the mountains. But I'll give myself the fun of gradually dressing in the local garb.

11 September, evening

Here I am in Roveredo, this is the crucial cut-off point. From the north down to here, there's a mix of German and Italian, now I've had a real Italian coachman. The innkeeper speaks no German and I must now practise my arts. How happy I am that the beloved language is now going to be the language of everyday use.

12 September, after supper

How I long to have you at my side for a moment, so that you could share my delight in the view that lies before me.

Today I could have been in Verona, but a fine effect of nature lay on my way, a beautiful spectacle of the *Lago di Garda*.

I didn't want to miss that, and am amply rewarded. Off from Roveredo after five and up a side valley that pours its waters into the *Adige*.* When you get up there, there's an enormous barrier blocking off the far end that you have to get over to get down to the lake. Here I saw the most splendid limestone rocks for picturesque studies.

As you come down, there's a small hamlet at the northern end of the lake with a small harbour or rather an access to the water, called *Torbole*. The fig trees had been getting more frequent on the way here, and climbing down I came across the first olive trees, which were thick with fruit. Here for the first time I found the white figs Countess Lanthieri promised me,* growing as a common fruit. From the room I'm sitting in, a door opens down into the yard, I put my table out there and drew you the view in a few strokes. It shows the lake all down its length, you can't see the end of it, especially on the left side.

After midnight the wind blows north to south, so anybody who wants to sail down the lake has to do it before daybreak, a few hours after sunrise it turns and blows northwards. Now since noon it's blowing very hard in my face and keeping me splendidly cool despite the hot sunshine.

I've just learned from Volkmann,* whom I've taken out of my case for the first time, that this lake was formerly called *Benacus*, and he points out a verse of Virgil's where it's mentioned:

teque
Fluctibus et fremitu assurgens Benace marino.*

The first Latin verse whose subject is there live before my eyes, and it proves very true as the wind rises and the lake gets choppy. I'll close now, take a walk when it gets cool, leave here at three in the morning, and then write to you again from Verona. The loveliest and grandest sights of nature are now behind me, now it's on to art, Antiquity, and lakeside life. Farewell! Today I did some work on Iphigenie, it went very well with the lake there before me. I must pack, and am loth to leave you, I'll think of you again today while drawing. The map of the Tyrol that I took from Knebel is enclosed, I've marked my route in pencil.

Written with the 46th parallel now behind me.

13 September

When you're dealing with water, you can't say: today I'll be in this or that place.

I'm in *Malcesine*, the first place in Venetian territory, on the eastern side of the lake. Now just a bit more about *Torbole*, the harbour where I stayed yesterday.

The inn has no locks on the doors, and the landlord said I could rest easy, even if everything I had with me was diamonds. Then the rooms have no windows, just frames with oil-paper in and yet they're delightful to be in, thirdly no lavatory. So you see one gets pretty close to the state of nature here. When I arrived and asked one of the servants where there was a convenience, he pointed down into the courtyard: *qui abasso! puo servirsi.* I asked him: *dove?* he answered *per tutto, dove vuol.** Everything's very happy-go-lucky, but it's all activity and life and all day long the women of the neighbourhood keep up their chattering and shouting, they're always making or doing something, I have yet to see a woman idle.

Delicious trout (*trutte*) are caught near *Torbole*, where the stream comes down from the mountains and the fish are looking for the way up. The Emperor gets 10 thousand florins rent for the rights.

They aren't real trout, they weigh up to 50 pounds, and have coloured spots all over their bodies right up to the head. The taste is something between trout and salmon, very delicate and excellent.

But what I'm really revelling in is the fruit: I eat figs all day. You can imagine how good the pears must be here, where there are already lemons growing. This morning I left Torbole at three with two men to row me, on and off the wind was in the right direction so we could use the sail, but we hadn't got much past Malcesine when the wind turned right about, and blew in its usual daytime direction due north. Rowing wasn't much use against this overwhelming force and we had to put in to the harbour at Malcesine.

It had been tranquil at dawn, with some fine clouds. I did a little drawing. We passed *Limona*, which has a neat and prosperous look, with terraced gardens up the mountainside where they grow lemon-trees. The whole garden consists of rows of square white stakes some distance apart laid out one behind the other up the slope, with the trees planted between them. Strong poles are laid across the top to cover them in winter, otherwise they'd get damaged even in this climate. There's a similar garden here in Malcesine, I'll have a go at drawing it.

And the castle too that stands by the water and makes a fine subject.

Going past earlier today I got a fair idea of it.

I felt frustrated this morning that I can't draw better, and glad that I can manage this much. Just as mineralogy too and my bit of botanical knowledge open up an immense amount for me and are the real value of the journey so far. Yesterday I put my overcoat away in my case, in Verona I must get myself something light to wear, it isn't exactly hot, but you feel warm really deep inside you, in a way that for ages I haven't had any conception of.

Evening.

My fancy of drawing the castle for you, which is a genuine counterpart to the Bohemian one, very nearly landed me in trouble. The inhabitants thought it was suspicious because this is where the frontier* runs and everyone's afraid of the Emperor. They mobbed me, but I did a fair imitation of Goodfriend,* I harangued and bewitched them. Details when we meet.

Left Malcesine on the 14th at 1 a.m., to catch the favourable wind, but didn't reach Bartolino till 10. Being sick of the mean little inns I hurried on, loaded my luggage on one mule and me on another, and arrived in Verona just before 1 p.m. on 14 September in tremendous heat. I'll write this, finish and bind the second Section, and go and see the amphitheatre.

It's impossible to convey in words what this place is like, it's just one large garden nearly five miles long and the same broad, I'm understating if anything, and lies very flat and very neatly laid out at the foot of the high ranges and cliffs. More detailed description in the next Section. A word more on my lake trip, it all ended happily and the splendour of the lake itself and the shores we passed, especially just by Brescia, gave me a real deep contentment. Where the mountains are no longer steep on the western side and the country gets flatter near the lake, there's a whole string of places it takes an hour and a half to sail past, *Gargnano, Bojaco, Cecine, Toscolan,*

Maderno, Verdom, Saló. Most of them are spread a good way along the bank too.

I could go on and on about all this beauty.

From Bartolino I made my way over a ridge that separates the valley the *Adige* runs through from the basin in which the lake lies.

The waters from the two sides seem formerly to have worked against each other and piled up this gigantic heap of gravel. Fertile soil has been deposited on top of it, but the people who till the fields have dreadful problems with the stones that keep coming up to the surface.

They have a good trick of building them up and making thick walls with them alongside the path.

And the mulberry trees at this height don't look so happy, for lack of moisture. There's no chance of springs up here, from time to time you find a puddle of rainwater that the mules quench their thirst from, and so do their drivers. Down by the river they've fitted up irrigation wheels so they can give the plantations that lie further back as much water as they like.

Supplement a
Weather

I give such a lot of attention to this point because I really believe that this is the region our sad northern fate depends on. As I said in the preceding Section. I don't really wonder that we have such bad summers, in fact I'm more puzzled how we can ever have good ones.

The night of the 9th to the 10th was alternately bright and overcast, the moon had a halo round it all the time. Towards 5 in the morning the whole sky was covered in cloud, grey but not trailing low and heavy.

The upper air was still sufficiently elastic, as the day went on the clouds split up, or in the terms of my theory: they were consumed, and the lower we got, the finer the weather was.

And as for Botzen, where the great bulk of the mountains still lay to the north, the air got more and more pure. Though I'd better put that more precisely.

You could see from the bands of landscape as they receded into the distance that the air was full of vapour, but the atmosphere was elastic enough to carry it.

As I came down lower, I could see that all the vapours from the Botzen valley and all the clouds coming up from the hills to the south were being drawn toward the mountain range and not covering it but wrapping it in a kind of height haze. In fact, I could see over the mountains in the far distance the unclear foot of a rainbow.

From all this I conclude that you will now be having changeable weather but with more good days than bad, for although the atmosphere as I keep on saying seems to stay elastic enough, still so much of the vapour must drift north where it can't be dissolved, and floating in a lower atmosphere it has to fall as rain. South of Botzen they've had the most beautiful weather all summer. A bit of dampness now and then (they say *Aqua* for gentle rain) and then sunshine again, even yesterday there were some drops of rain now and then, and the sun kept shining with it. The landlord's daughter has just been telling me it's a long time since they had such a good year, everything's doing well. And I believe it, precisely because we've had such a bad one.

Supplement d[1]
Mountain and Rock Types

A quarter of an hour from the Brenner there's a marble quarry, it was already getting dusk. Like the limestone I noted on the other side, it can and must be lying on top of the mica schist[2] with limestone alongside (I wouldn't quite say alternating).

Near Colman when it got light I found mica schist, even in the river I didn't find any limestone (it's possible I missed it, also it crumbles more easily, perhaps there's not even much of that). Below Colman the porphyries started, which I'm bringing a collection of, so I won't describe them. The rocks were so splendid, and the heaps by the roadside so temptingly ready broken up that on the spot you could have made and packed a Voigt study set.* There's no problem about taking any piece of stone I want with me, if I can only tone down my eye and appetite to a smaller scale.

Soon after Colmann I came across a porphyry rock that split into very regular plates.

---

[1] See Färber's *Journey to Italy*, p. 397. Haquet's *Journey through the . . . Alps.* (G.)

[2] Färber calls it horn schist, but the terminology of rock types was vaguer then than it is now. See Färber's laments, pp. 400 ff. (G.)

Before getting to Botzen a porphyry with green flecks of soapstone and a soapstone detachment.

Below Botzen porphyries, finally between Brandsol and Neumarck the porphyry that splits into regular plates and, if you like, into columns with a parallelepiped-shaped base.

Färber thought they were volcanic products, but that was 14 years ago, when the whole science was newer. Haquet has a go at him for it.

List of the rock types I've collected

1. Normal grey limestone before and around Inspruck.
2. Gneiss from the roadstones approaching the Brenner.
3. Gneiss type from the same.
4. The same with clearer traces of feldspar outcropping down by the lake.
5. Mica schist with quartz and yellowish-grey calcite.
6. The same with limestone.
7. Limestone in the form found on top of mica schist.
8. The same at the detachment, belongs by rights further up the list.
9. Mica schist on limestone.
10. Slaty limestone from the region.
11. Marble below the Brenner on the Sterzing side.
12. Granite from the road below Kolman.
13. Gneiss specimen from the same.
14–18. Porphyry specimens from the same.
19. A porphyry that splits regularly.
20. Porphyry with green talc or soapstone flecks outside Botzen.
21. Porphyry mentioned by Färber, below Brandsol.
22. Limestone further down into the valley.
23. Basalt found as gravel on the way from Roveredo to Torbole.
24. Granite debris from the *Lago di Garda*.

Supplement e
People

From the very start of the day coming down from the Brenner I noticed a strange alteration in their physical appearance.

Particularly the women had a brownish pallid complexion, miserable facial features, and the children just the same and pitiable to see. The men were a bit better, with good regular features, I wondered what the cause might be, and thought perhaps it was the diet of maize and buckwheat. My notion has been confirmed more and more. The maize, which they call yellow polenta from the colour of the grain, and the black polenta are ground, then the flour is boiled up into a thick porridge and eaten like that. The *Germans*, that is on the other side of the mountains, pluck the dough apart and fry it in butter; but the Tyrolean Italians eat it as it is, sometimes with grated cheese on top, and no meat from one year's end to the next, that must necessarily gum up and clog all their vessels, especially the women and children, and that accounts for the whole unhealthy complexion. I asked whether there weren't any rich peasants.—Yes, of course. Don't they ever give themselves a treat? don't they eat better?—No, they're just used to it.—So what do they do with their money? What other costs do they have?—Oh, don't worry, they have their masters who take it* off them.

That was the sum total of the conversation with my landlord's daughter, a very pleasant body.

Otherwise they eat only fruit, and green beans boiled and dressed with garlic and oil.

The people I met from the towns looked healthier, and there were certainly girls with pretty faces and round cheeks both in the country and the small towns, but they were an exception.

When there's a plentiful wine year, the townspeople and other dealers buy it off the peasants dirt cheap and sell it on. *Pauper ubique jacet.** And the *sub*-owner is everywhere done down. In Trent I had a close look at the people, they have an altogether better look than in the country. The women are mostly a bit too short for their girth and the size of their heads, but often quite pretty and obliging faces. The male faces as above, but here they look less fresh than the women, probably because the women do more physical work and get more exercise, the men being merchants or craftsmen sit around more. On the *Lago di Garda* I found the people very brown in complexion without any reddish colouring; they didn't look unhealthy though, but quite fresh and easy.

THIRD SECTION

VERONA, VICENZA, PADUA

Verona, 15 September, evening

Yes, my beloved, I've finally arrived where I should have been long ago, many things in my destiny would have been easier. Yet who can really say, and to tell the honest truth: I couldn't rightly have wanted it earlier, not even half a year earlier.

You can see the format of my diary is changing and the content will change too. I'll go on writing conscientiously, but if you'll get Volkmann's *Journey to Italy*, from the Library perhaps, I'll give the page references and proceed on the assumption you've read the book.

I've been here since midday yesterday, and have already seen and learnt a lot. I'll gradually get my thoughts down on paper.

16 September

I'm gradually adjusting. I let it all happen just as it comes, and soon I will have recovered from the leap over the mountains. I just wander round in my usual way taking a quiet look at everything, and I receive and retain a good impression.

Now things in order as I saw them:

The Amphitheatre

The first monument of ancient times that I've seen and that has stayed so well preserved, has *been* so well preserved. A book that I'm sending gives a good idea of it.

When you go in, or stand on the top rim, it's an odd impression, of something grand and yet there's really nothing to see. Nor should it be seen empty, but packed full of people, as the Emperor and the Pope* saw it. But it only had its effect in those times when the people were more of a 'people' than they are now. For actually an amphitheatre like this is designed to impress the people with themselves, to give them the illusion they're important.

If there's something happening on the flat and everyone comes running to see what's up, the ones at the back try every possible way to get a look-in over the heads of the ones in front, they roll barrels up, drive carts up, put planks across this way and that, bring up benches, they crowd on to a nearby rise, and before you know where you are a bowl's been formed. When actors come, or if there's going to be a bullfight, there'll be some kind of platform put up on one side for those who can pay, the common sort have to manage as best they can.

This general need is what the architect has to cater for, he makes an artificial version of a bowl, as simple as he possibly can, and the ornamentation is the people themselves. As I said just now, when they see themselves all gathered together, they can't but be amazed. Whereas mostly their experience of themselves is of everyone running this way and that in a turmoil with no kind of order and certainly no discipline, the many-headed, many-minded, wavering, vacillating beast finds itself turned into a single whole, tuned to a unity, connected and confirmed as a mass, and as if animated into one form by one spirit. The simplicity of the oval is felt in the most pleasant way possible by every eye, and every head serves as the measure of how large the whole thing is. Now, seeing it empty, you don't have any scale, you don't even know whether it's large or small.

Being built of a slow-weathering marble, it's well preserved.

On the following points when we meet.

Piece of the outer wall.

Did it go all the way round?

Arcades round the outside let to craftsmen, 20 to 30 florins a section.

'Ballon'

As I was leaving the *Arena* (which is what they call the amphitheatre) a mile or so further on I came upon a public match. Four Veronese gentlemen were playing a ball-game against four visitors. It's a regular thing among themselves all year round, an hour or two before nightfall. This time, as there was a visiting team, an incredible local crowd had gathered, there could well have been four to five thousand men watching (I didn't see women, of any social class). A moment ago, talking about the needs of the spectators when something worth watching takes place on the flat, I was describing just the sort of chance natural amphitheatre in which I saw the people built up above each other here. You could hear from some way off the enthusiastic applause that greeted every significant shot. The rest when we meet.

Porta stupa or *del Palio*

The most beautiful gate, permanently shut. Only when you get a few hundred paces away from it do you recognize what a fine building it is. But as a gate, and for the great distance from which you have to see it, it isn't well conceived.

People give you various reasons why it's blocked, I have a conjecture. The artist plainly intended this gate to give the Corso a new layout, for it stands at the wrong angle to the present street; the left-hand side is just a row of hovels, but the right-angle line at the centre is aimed straight at a nunnery that would have had to be flattened, they realized that, what's more the local gentry had no inclination to build in that direction, the architect died and so they blocked up the gate and that was that.

Now a word that applies to works of the ancients in general.

The artist had a grand idea to execute, a major need to satisfy, or perhaps just a true idea to execute, and he could be grand and true in the execution if he was the right artist for the job. But if the need is a small one, if the basic idea is untrue, what's a great artist doing there and what is he to make out of it? He works his fingers to the bone treating the small subject in the grand manner and something does come of it, but a monstrosity whose origins are plain to see.

NB This remark just chances to be here and has no connection with what went before.

Theatre and Museum

The theatre building has a fine grand portal with six Ionian columns. Above the entrance you see through between the two middle columns to the marble bust of Maffei* in front of a painted niche carried by two painted Corinthian columns. That Maffei had the bust removed in his lifetime I put down more to his good taste than his modesty, for the bust doesn't belong there, nor does anyone else's, certainly not just stuck on instead of being inset in the wall, with a great wig to boot. If only he'd found himself a good spot in one of the rooms where the pictures of the Philharmonic Society hang and got his friends to put up his picture there when he died, good taste would have been served and it would also look more republican.

But if people had really wanted to do that, they would have had to give the entrance a solid surround and not a decoration of painted columns, open a niche in the wall, leave off the wig, and make a colossal bust, and with all that I doubt that they'd have been able to force this whole part to harmonize with the large columns. But harmony of this kind doesn't seem to interest the Philharmonic gentlemen much.

Thus the gallery that frames the forecourt is equally small in conception and the fluted Doric dwarfs make a miserable showing beside the smooth Ionic giants. Still, we'll excuse that in view of the fine institute that is housed below these galleries, and also considering that architecture is a very tricky problem—if immense amounts aren't spent on a little, it can achieve nothing. More another time.

Now back to the antiquities that are contained beneath the galleries.

They're largely bas-reliefs, which were also mostly found in the area round Verona (indeed, they even say in the Arena) which I just don't understand. They're Etruscan, Greek, and Roman pieces from the less good periods, and more modern ones.

The bas-reliefs are set in the wall and have the numbers they were given by Maffei in the work that describes them. Altars and column fragments etc. stand in the spaces between the columns.

There are very good, excellent pieces among them, and even the less good things bear witness to a magnificent age. The wind that blows from the graves of the ancients comes with fragrances as from a hill of roses.

Notably there is a quite splendid triolith of white marble with Genii, which Raphael* imitated and transfigured in the lunettes of his Story of Psyche. I recognized them at once. And the grave monuments are warm and touching. You see a man beside his wife looking out of a niche as if from a window, a father and mother stand with their son between them and look at one another with ineffable naturalness, a couple stretch out their hands to each other. A father seems to be taking a calm leave of his family on his deathbed. We'll go through the engravings together. I was so deeply moved in the presence of these stones that I could not hold back my tears. Here is no man in armour on his knees waiting for a joyous resurrection, what the artist has here set down with more or less skill is never anything more than the simple present of human beings, which thereby prolongs their existence and makes it permanent. They don't put their hands together, they don't look up to heaven; rather they are what they were, they stand together, they feel for each other, they love one another, and that is expressed in the stone most delightfully, often with a certain technical clumsiness. The engravings often undo that effect, they beautify, but the spirit has flown. There's a very fine bronze here of the well-known Diomede with the image of Pallas Athene.

Looking at the grave monuments I thought a lot about Herder.* In so many ways I wish I had him with me.

There's also an ornamented column in white marble, very rich and in good taste.

My eye is only gradually getting used to all these things, I just write them down as each one strikes me.

Tomorrow I'm going to see it all again and write you a few more words.

Cathedral

The Titian* is very blackened and apparently it's a picture from his least good period.

I like the way he makes Mary, as she's taken up into heaven, look not upwards but downwards, in the direction of her friends.

St *Giorgio*

A gallery of good pictures. The altarpieces, if not all equally good, still all remarkable.

But the unfortunate artists, what were they given to paint? and for whom.

A rain of manna, 30 feet across and 20 high, the miracle of the 5 loaves as a companion-piece. What was there to paint in that. Hungry human beings falling over themselves for crumbs, countless others being given bread. The artists tortured themselves to give such miserable subjects some kind of significance.

One of them [Caroto] who had to paint St Ursula and the eleven thousand virgins for an altarpiece got out of the difficulty with great good sense. The figure of St Ursula has something strangely virginal without any charm.

I'd never stop, so let's talk about something else.

People

You see the people on the go all the time here, and in some streets where there are shops and craftsmen's booths they make an entertaining spectacle. For there isn't just a doorway into the shop or workshop, no, the whole breadth of the house is open, you see everything that's going on in there, the tailors all sewing and the cobblers making shoes half in the street. The booths are part of the street. In the evening when the lights are lit, it's all full of life.

The squares are packed on market-days. Vegetables and fruit as far as the eye can see. Garlic and onions galore. And then they're shouting, singing, and larking about all day long, scrapping, throwing themselves around, laughing and cheering without cease.

With the climate mild, and food freely available, the living is easy, everyone who can be is out of doors. At night the singing and the racket start up with a vengeance. You hear 'Marlborough'* sung everywhere you go. Then a zither, a violin, they all whistle and do bird-imitations, you hear sounds you wouldn't dream of. A mild climate gives even the poor a good feeling about their existence, and makes even the shadier elements among the people respectable.

The grubbiness and lack of comfort indoors has the same origin. They're too carefree to think about things like that. For the people anything goes, the middling class live from day to day too, only the rich and the nobility keep up any standards. Though I don't know how things look inside their palazzi. The forecourts, arcades, etc. are all filthy with refuse, and that's quite natural, you just have to see it from the people's angle. They feel they have prior rights. The rich man can be rich and build palaces, the *nobile* is free to rule, but if he puts up an arcade or a forecourt, then the people use it for their necessities and no necessity is more urgent than to get rid as fast as they can of what they consume as much of as they can.

Anybody who doesn't want that mustn't play the great lord; that is to say, he mustn't behave as if a part of his dwelling-place were a public space, he has to shut his door and then everything's clear. With public buildings, the people won't be done out of their due. And that's the way it is everywhere in Italy.

One more observation that isn't easy to make—

And meanwhile my supper's been served, I feel tired and written out, for I've had pen in hand the whole day. Now I've got to copy out Iphigenie myself and get these pages in shape for you. For now good night, my dearest. Tomorrow or when the spirit will, my observation.

16 September evening 10 o'clock.

17th, evening

If only everything I've done today were already down on paper. It's 8 o'clock (*una doppo notte**) and I've run my legs off, now quickly, everything just as it comes. Today I went walking through the town and on the Brà* quite unobserved. I made a note of the way a certain middling sort of people dress here and got myself up exactly the same. I get tremendous fun out of that. Now I also imitate their ways. For example, they all fling their arms out when walking. People of a certain class only do it with the right arm because they wear swords and are therefore accustomed to keep the left arm still, others do it with both arms and so on.

It's incredible what a sharp eye the people have for anything foreign. So they couldn't get over my boots in the first few days, as these are expensive items, not worn even in winter here; but what really struck me was this morning, when they were all going about with flowers, garlic, etc., they didn't fail to notice a cypress branch I'd picked in the garden and that my companion had in his hand (there were green cones on it, and he also had a little twig of the capers that grow on the city wall). Everybody, big and small, looked at what he was carrying and wondered why.

I brought these twigs from the Giusti garden which is splendidly situated and has enormous cypresses, all sticking up like needles into the sky. (The yews cut to a point in northern gardens are an imitation of the beauty that grows naturally here.) A tree whose branches from top to bottom and from the oldest to the youngest all strive skywards, that goes on growing for 300 years (the date the garden was established suggests they're older than that) surely deserves to be revered.

They are mostly still green all the way up, and more of them would be if people had checked the growth of the ivy in time before it got a grip on many of them and suffocated the lower branches.

I found capers in bloom hanging down from the wall and a beautiful *mimosa*. Laurels in the hedges, etc.

The garden design is mediocre, not grand enough in relation to the hill whose flank it goes up. Really only the cypresses balance the rocks. More another time when we get on to other gardens.

I've seen the *Fiera*,* which is a really fine institution.

Then the gallery of the Palazzo Gherardini, where there are some fine things by Orbetto.* From a distance you only get to know a few masters, and even those often only by name, when you get closer to this firmament, and those of the second and third magnitude also start twinkling and every one is a star too, then suddenly the world is wide and art is rich. Except that the painters are often unfortunate with their subjects. And the pieces with several figures so rarely come off. I found the best composition here a Samson sleeping in Delilah's lap, she's just quietly reaching across for the scissors. The idea and the execution are very good. The rest I'll say no more about.

In the Palazzo Canossa there was a striking Danae,* which I just mention. Beautiful fish from Bolca.*

I went to the Museum again. What I said about the colonnade and the bust of Maffei requires some modification.

Of the antiquities I'll say nothing, there are copper engravings of those, when I see them again it will all come back to me. The beautiful triolith is alas slowly decaying, it's exposed to the evening sun and the evening wind, if only they would put a wooden casing over it. The half-finished palace of the city governor would have been a fine piece of architecture if it had been completed.

Otherwise the Nobili are still building a lot, unfortunately they all build on the spot where their palazzo already stands, that is, often in the narrow lanes. Thus someone is building a magnificent seminary façade in a narrow alley in the remote outskirts. This evening I went to the amphitheatre again. I have to educate my eye first and get used to seeing things. What I said the first time was confirmed. And the Veronese really do deserve praise for the way they maintain it. The steps or seats seem almost all new. There's an inscription in honour of one *Hieronymus Maurigenus* and his unbelievable industry.

I walked along the edge of the bowl up on the top step at sunset waiting for night (*Notte*, the 24th hour). I was quite alone and down below on the broad stones of the Brà, great crowds of people were promenading, men of all classes, women of the middle class.

Here a word on the *zendale* that they wear and the *veste*. It's just the right costume for a people who don't bother about always being cleanly, and yet often want to appear in public, in church, on the corso. The *veste* is a black taffeta skirt that is thrown over other skirts. If the woman has a clean one (usually white) on underneath, she has the trick of hitching up one side of the black one. This black skirt is so arranged that it separates the waist and covers the panels of the bodice. The bodice can be of any colour. The *zendale* is a big cap with long bands, they keep the cap high over the head with a contraption of wires and the bands are joined in the manner of a sash, at the back of the body, and the ends trail down behind.

Casa Bevi l'aqua

Beautiful, splendid things.

A Paradise by Tintoretto,* or rather the coronation of the Virgin as Queen of Heaven in the presence of all the patriarchs, prophets, saints, angels, etc., a senseless conception carried through with absolute genius. Such lightness of brush, spirit, and richness of expression that you would have to own the picture yourself to fully admire and enjoy it, for infinite artistry went into it, and the very last angels' heads have such character, the biggest figures are at most a foot high, Mary and Christ, who is placing the crown on her head, are perhaps about 4 inches tall. But Eve is the handsomest woman in the whole picture and still in the old way a touch lascivious.

A couple of portraits by Paolo Veronese* have only increased my high regard for this artist.

The antiquities are fine. I greatly liked an Endymion.* The busts, mostly with restored noses, very interesting. An Augustus with the Corona civica.* A Caligula, etc.

Clock

So you can more easily understand the Italian clock, I've devised the visual aid that follows.

Comparative Circle of the Italian and German Clock, with the Italian-style times for the second half of September

Midday

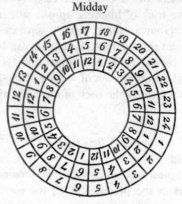

Midnight

Night increases half an hour every half-month				Day increases half an hour every half-month			
Month	Day	Nightfall by our reckoning	Midnight is then at	Month	Day	Nightfall by our reckoning	Midnight is then at
Aug.	1	$8\frac{1}{2}$	$3\frac{1}{2}$	Feb.	1	$5\frac{1}{2}$	$6\frac{1}{2}$
—	15	8	4	—	15	6	6
Sept.	1	$7\frac{1}{2}$	$4\frac{1}{2}$	Mar.	1	$6\frac{1}{2}$	$5\frac{1}{2}$
—	15	7	5	—	15	7	5
Oct.	1	$6\frac{1}{2}$	$5\frac{1}{2}$	Apr.	1	$7\frac{1}{2}$	$4\frac{1}{2}$
—	15	6	6	—	15	8	4
Nov.	1	$5\frac{1}{2}$	$6\frac{1}{2}$	May	1	$8\frac{1}{2}$	$3\frac{1}{2}$
—	15	5	7	—	15	9	3

From that point, times don't change and it is:

	Night at	Midnight at		Night at	Midnight at
Dec. Jan. }	5	7	June July }	9	3

From that point, times don't change and it is:

The inner circle is our 24 hours from midnight round to midnight again, divided into twice twelve as we reckon and our clocks show. The middle circle shows what the clocks strike here in this season of

the year, that is also twice twelve, only in such a way that what's
1 o'clock here would be 8 o'clock at home, and so on right through
the twelve. At 8 a.m. as we would call it, it strikes one again here, and
so forth.

The outer circle shows how they really count up to 24. If I hear it
strike 7 in the night, and I know that midnight is at 5, I subtract
$(7 - 5 = 2)$ which is 2 hours after midnight. If I hear it strike 7
during the day, then I know that midnight is at 5, and so is noon
by the clock, then I perform the same operation as before
$(7 - 5 = 2)$ so it's 2 hours after noon. If however I want to say it,
then I need to know that noon is at 17 hours, so I now add
$(17 + 2 = 19)$ and say nineteen hours, if I want to say what with us
would be two.[1]

When you've read that and taken a look at my table, it will make
your head swim to start with, and you'll exclaim 'How dreadfully
inconvenient!',* and yet on the spot it's not only something you soon
get used to, you actually get quite a lot of fun out of it, as the people
do, for whom the endless calculating and comparing this way and
that is an occupation in itself. They're always waving their hands
around in the air anyway, working things out in their heads, and they
enjoy messing about with numbers.

But now comes the main point. In a country where people enjoy
the daytime but especially look forward to the evening, the point
when it becomes *night* is extremely significant. When the day's work
ends. When people have to start their stroll or come back home.
When night falls, fathers want their daughters back indoors and so
on, night concludes evening and ends the day. And what a *day* means
is something that we Cimmerians* in our eternal mists and gloom
scarcely know, it's all one to us whether it's day or night, for when
can we ever enjoy ourselves in the open air? Here when night comes,
the day's gone, another 24 hours have passed, the rosary is said, and a
new calculation begins. That changes with each new season, and the
coming of night always draws a noticeable line, someone who *lives*
here can't fail to notice.

It would be taking a great deal from the people if the German-
style clock were to be forced on them, or rather, you simply cannot

---

[1] NB the locals don't bother much about noon and midnight, they just count, for the
evening when it strikes, the hours as they strike; and in the daytime when it strikes, they
add the number on to 12. (G.)

and must not take anything away from people which is so intimately interwoven with their nature.

An hour or an hour and a half before night the nobility start driving out. They make for the Brà, the long broad thoroughfare that runs to the Porta nuova, out of the gate and round the town walls, and when the clocks strike night everyone turns back, partly they drive to the churches to say the *Ave Maria della sera*,* partly they stop on the Brà and the ladies accept the attentions of cavaliers who come up to the coaches and then it's a lengthy business, I've never waited to see the outcome. But people go on walking about there far into the night.

It had just rained and laid the dust, it was really a lively and jolly sight.

Weather

It thundered and lightened and rained for fully twelve hours, then it was fine and clear again. In general people here too complain about a bad summer. They may not have had quite such a good one as in other years, but I also notice that they're pretty demanding. Beause they're used to good weather and everyone goes about in shoes and stockings and light clothes, they curse and swear straight away when there's a bit of wind and rain, where we'd be glad to have so little of it.

I noticed after the rain that the clouds soon moved across against the Tyrolean mountains and stayed there, and it didn't altogether clear up. The whole system is now shifting northwards and will give you some dismal cold days.

The rain and clouds we get here are probably from the Po valley, or from further away over the sea and so it goes on as I spelled out in full detail in my last.

Also worth noting

how beautiful the outside of the porta *del Pallio* is.

The dark antiquity of the church of St Zeno, the patron saint of the city, a comfortable laughing saint.

The lizards weaving about in the evening sun on the steps of the amphitheatre.

I thought I'd made a wonderful job of explaining the Italian clock to you, but I realize my method wasn't the best. Still, the circle diagram and the table beneath it are at any rate better than my explanation and will serve for the future.

List of rock-types collected on the way

Verona
26. Red Veronese marble.
27. Bronzino.
28. White limestone they carve statues from.
29. Pieces of basalt debris.

Vicenza
30. Lava from *Monte Berico*.
31. Limestone from there.
32. Limestone they make fine slabs from in Vicenza.
33. Limestone that they saw up and cut to all sorts of shapes.
34. Basalt from which they cut beautiful slabs for the floors of entrance halls, the smaller pieces are used for other kinds of paving.
35. A lava that they also cut into slabs.

Vicenza 19 Sept.

I arrived here a few hours ago and have already done a quick tour of the town, seen the Teatro Olimpico and the buildings by Palladio.* You can get the engravings from the Library, so I won't say anything or name anything except in general terms.

If you don't see these works on the spot, you can have no real conception of them. Palladio was a great man through a deep inner quality that comes out in everything he did.

The greatest difficulty is always how to use the orders of columns in a modern building. Combining columns and walls harmoniously is almost impossible, more on that when I'm back. But how he mingled them, how impressive his buildings are when they're there in front of you, he makes you forget they're monstrosities! There really is something divine in his talents, it's absolutely the power of a great poet who takes truth and untruth and makes some third thing from them that entrances us. The Teatro Olimpico, as you may know, is a realization of an ancient theatre. It is beyond description beautiful. But as a theatre, compared with our present-day ones, it seems to me like an aristocratic, rich, well-educated child, contrasted with a shrewd merchant who is neither so aristocratic, rich, nor well-educated, but has a better idea of what he can do with the means at his disposal. If you set beside it the limited, dirty needs of human beings, the way the abilities of impresarios mostly fell short of the architects' conceptions, and how ill-matched these delightful monuments of the human spirit are to run-of-the-mill humanity,* then you realize that it's just the same as in the moral world. You earn little thanks from people if you set out to raise their inner needs to a higher plane, give them a grand idea of themselves, and make them feel the splendour of a great true existence (and that is what Palladio's works do, directly and sensuously, in high degree); but if you trick the Birds,* tell them tales, help them along from day to day and so on, then you're their man and that's why so many churches came into being, because the needs of mortals are best catered for from that angle. I don't say that to belittle my friends,* I only say that's what people are like, and that we mustn't be surprised if everything is the way it is.

The effect of Palladio's basilica when you see it standing beside an old castle-like structure dotted with different-sized windows, which—tower and all—he no doubt simply pretended wasn't there, is beyond words.

The way here from Verona is very pleasant, you travel north-west along the line of the mountains and have the foothills of limestone, sandstone, clay, always on your left; on the hills formed by these rocks there are settlements, castles, houses, then there's the wide plain that you drive through. The straight, well-maintained broad highway runs through fertile fields, there are rows of trees with vines trained up into them so that they trail down as if they were branches. You get an idea where decorative festoons came from. The grapes are early, they weigh down the tendrils that trail down long and swaying, there are all sorts and conditions of people thronging the road, I especially liked the carts pulled by four oxen with great vats in which the grapes are brought from the vineyards and trodden, the drivers were mostly standing in them and it looked exactly like Bacchus in a triumphal chariot. Between the rows of vines the soil is used for all kinds of local cereal crops, especially maize and *sorgo*.* As you get near Vicenza there are more hills, running north to south, volcanic ones, closing off the plain, and Vicenza lies at their foot, in a sort of bay.

20 Sept. evening half-past 8, by local time half-past 1

Yesterday there was an opera, it lasted beyond midnight and I was longing for my bed. The subject was patched together from the *Three Sultanas* and the *Abduction from the Seraglio*,* the music was easy listening but probably by an amateur, not a new idea that struck me anywhere in the whole piece. The ballet sections on the other hand were quite delightful, I kept thinking of Stein* and wishing he could enjoy them too. The principal pair danced an allemande that couldn't have been more delicate. You see, I'm gradually being prepared, there'll be better to come. You can imagine that I collected a good deal for my Wilhelm novel. It's a really fine new theatre,* magnificent in a modest way and in a uniform style as befits a real *town*, only the box for the *Capitan grande** has a longer drape or tapestry hanging down in front. The prima donna is a great favourite with the populace. When she comes on they clap like mad and the Birds are quite beside themselves for joy when she does something really special, as she often does. She's a pleasant body, has a pretty figure, a fine voice, a pleasing face, and a very decent manner; only her arm movements could be a bit more graceful.

But still, I shan't be coming again. I feel I'm past being a Bird myself.

On the other hand, I've once more spent the day revelling in Palladio's works. And I'm not going to get away soon, I can already tell that and am letting things take their course. I have plenty of work to do on Iphigenie and copying the text out. It hardly matters where I do that, and better here than in some place where I'd be engulfed in noise and bustle.

I have to give it to the people of Vicenza that you enjoy the privileges of a big town with them, they don't stare at you no matter what you do, but with that they're quite chatty and obliging, etc.

I find the womenfolk especially very pleasing. Nothing against the Verona women, they have well-shaped, prominent features but mostly pallid, and the *zendale* does them no favours because you expect something beautiful under the beautiful costume.

But here I find a great many pretty persons, particularly the dark-haired ones appeal to me, there's a blonde type too that I somehow don't feel comfortable with.

What I like is a generally free and easy manner, because everybody is constantly out in the open air and lounging about, people get to be easy with one another. Today in the church of the *Madonna del Monte* I had a nice encounter, but couldn't follow it up.

This evening I walked about the square for an hour and a half till it was quite dark. There's no getting away from it, the basilica is a magnificent work, impossible to conceive if you haven't seen it in reality, the four columns on the palace of the *Capitan* are marvellous too. The square between these two buildings is only forty paces across and they only look all the more magnificent for it. I'll tell you more about that when I'm back, for it's all been described and engraved two or three times over, so there's plenty to remind me. I'm also enclosing two small volumes for your edification.

I also saw the celebrated Rotonda today, the country house of the Marchese Capri, here the architect was free to do whatever he liked and he almost went a bit too far. But it was one more occasion for me to admire his towering genius. His design was meant to add something to the whole scene, from a distance it looks quite delightful, close up I do have a few humble objections.

I wish to heaven Palladio had done a design for the Madonna *del Monte* and good Christian souls had executed it, then we'd really see something which, as things are, we have no conception of.

Now a word about the views. The Rotonda is located just where such a building belongs, the view is unimaginably beautiful, once again I don't want to describe. Vicenza as a whole is magnificently situated and I'd very much like to stay here for a spell, though of course not in an inn, but properly settled somewhere and then just take it easy, the air is splendid and healthy.

21st, evening

Today I called on the old architect Scamozzi* who published an edition of Palladio's buildings and is an excellent man. He gave me some useful pointers. Tomorrow I'm driving out to see a country house belonging to *Conte Tiene.*

Perhaps you remember that among Palladio's buildings there's one that's just called *la Casa di Palladio*, I always had a particular liking for it; but when you see it close up, it's a great deal more, it really comes home to you how much better it is than you were able to realize. When I get back there'll be a lot to say about that. If it didn't make a stir and compromise my incognito as nobody special,

I'd have it drawn and illuminated just as it stands with some of the neighbouring houses.

I keep just walking about everywhere, looking at things and training my eye and responses. I'm feeling well too, and in a very relaxed mood. My observations of individuals and the crowd, the state and its government, nature and art, customs and history go on all the time, and without feeling in the least stretched I get immense enjoyment and worthwhile reflection out of it. You know how the presence of things speaks to me, and here I'm in conversation with things all day long. I'm living very frugally. I can't take the local red wine, that's been true all the way down from the Tyrol, I drink it generously mixed with water like St Louis,* just a pity I'm too old for sainthood.

Today I also called on Dr Tura. For something like five years he applied himself passionately to botany, collected a *herbarium* of the *flora* of Italy, and in the last bishop's time laid out a Botanical Garden. But that's all vanished; medical practice drove out natural history, the *herbarium* is being eaten by the worms, the bishop is dead, and the Botanical Garden, as is only proper, has been put down to cabbages and garlic again. Dr Tura is a cultured man, he told me his story in a totally open, modest, unaffected way, spoke altogether very precisely and obligingly too, but didn't feel inclined to open up his cabinets, it was soon over and time for me to leave.

Towards evening I went back to the *Rotonda*, which is half an hour outside town, then to the *Madonna del Monte* and strolled through the market-hall down to my favourite square, bought a pound of grapes for 3 soldi, ate them sitting under Palladio's colonnades, and crept home as it was beginning to get dark and cool.

This evening there's another *opera*, but I can't make up my mind to suffer the *opus* again, although I'd be glad to see a new set of ballet scenes. Let's use the night for sleeping and make the most of the next day.

Here are the inscriptions from the Rotonda, as displayed on the four pediments:

Marcus Capra Gabrielis F.
Qui aedes has arctissimo primogeniturae gradui subjecit.
Una cum omnibus censibus agris vallibus et collibus
citra viam magnam
*Memoriae perpetuae mandans haec dum sustinet at abstinet.**

All of which, especially the ending, is a splendid text for future conversations.

22 Sept.

Still in Vicenza and probably here for a few days yet. If I could freely follow my own inclinations, I should dig in here for a month, do a quick course in architecture with Scamozzi, and then travel on well equipped. But that's more detail than my plan will allow and we want to be off again very soon.

This morning I was in *Tiene*, which lies to the north over towards the mountains, and where a new building has been put up based on an old design, an excellent work barring a few minor objections. It has an excellent position in a great plain with the limestone alps as a background and no foothills in between. From the castle all the way along the straight highway there is running water on both sides irrigating the wide rice-fields through which you drive.

This evening I was at a meeting held in the Academy of the Olympians.* Hilarious, but worthwhile all the same, it adds a bit of savour and activity to people's lives.

The room we met in is next door to Palladio's theatre, a nice interior, well lit, the Capitan and some of the nobility were present. And also an audience from the higher classes, a lot of priests, about five hundred people in all.

The President had set the theme: *has invention or imitation had the more beneficial effect in the arts?* You can see that, if the two are separated like that, the debate could go on for a hundred years. The gentlemen of the Academy duly made the most of the opportunity and put forward all sorts of views, in prose and verse, much of it very good. And in every way it was a lively gathering. The audience shouted bravo and clapped and laughed. If this were my nation and my language, I'd really stir them up.

You can imagine, Palladio was mentioned at every turn, and one man had the bright idea of saying that the others had got in first with Palladio, so he was going to talk up Francheschini (a big silk merchant), and he began spelling out the advantages that *imitating* the textiles of Lyons and Florence has had for Vicenza. You can imagine that gave rise to a lot of laughter.

In general, those who defended imitation got more applause, because they were saying all things that the great mass think and are up to thinking, although it was the weaker case. At one moment the audience gave extra hearty applause to some really crude sophistries. One man made some excellent points in favour of invention, but precisely that wasn't to the crowd's liking. I'm very glad to have seen all this too. Everything's going well for me, and it really is splendid to see Palladio revered as a great luminary by his compatriots after all this time. Lots more thoughts on this when we meet.

So far I've only seen the two Italian cities, *daughter*-cities* (not to say provincial cities) and have hardly talked to a single human being, but I already know my Italians pretty well. They're like our courtiers who think they're the top people in the world and, given the advantages they have, can happily go on imagining that with impunity.

But all in all a really good people, you only have to see the children and common folk as I now see them and am able to see them, because I'm constantly—and deliberately—exposed to contact with them.

When I'm back, you shall have the fullest descriptions of them, figures and faces and all.

For a long time I was inclined to make Verona or Vicenza Mignon's home background.* But now there's no doubt, it's Vicenza, that's another reason why I have to stay here for a few more days. Farewell. My scribbling's all over the place this evening, but something's better than nothing. Quills and ink and everything are hopelessly messy.

23 Sept.

I'm still stealing around, keeping my eyes skinned, and of course seeing daily more. Nothing now about buildings. When we look at the engravings together, then a great deal.

Fine weather these last few days, overcast and cool today, but none of that damp cold that's so murderous with us up north.

I'm now copying out my Iphigenie, that occupies a lot of my time. And yet here among an alien people and all the new sights, it gives me a certain special something and a feeling of contact with home.*

I'm going to throw away the Dedication to the German public that I'd begun, and do a new one as soon as Iphigenie's finished.

The women here are very neatly dressed. A white kerchief that the lower class wind round their heads and arrange like a veil doesn't do much for their faces, it takes a really pretty one not to be deprived of all effect by it. If you go into a dark church outside service times and see a couple of these veiled pious souls sitting or kneeling in there, it looks spooky enough.

The way the lower-class women tie their hair back and wind it into plaits is fine for the young ones but unsightly when they're older, it makes their hair come out and leaves the forehead bald.

The women carry baskets, buckets, or whatever on a bendy wooden yoke or bow.

They can quite easily manage even heavy things by catching hold of the handles too, as the above sketch shows. The people themselves, I'm sure, are good-hearted, I just look at the children and spend time among them, and the old folk too. Got up for the part, which also includes wearing linen netherstocks (this at once brings me down a few social notches) I stand around in the market-place among them, seize any occasion to talk, ask them things, watch how they behave among themselves, and can't sufficiently praise their naturalness, candour, and easy ways. I'll have more to say later, when we've seen more of them, about all this and how it relates to the common opinion of their cunning, mistrust of strangers, duplicity, and even violence.

I'm keeping very well and cheerful, just sometimes towards evening I have to watch out that I don't get a bit downcast and the longing for you and Fritz and Herder or some lesser sympathetic soul doesn't get the upper hand. But I keep it under control, make sure I have something to occupy me, and so it passes.

24 Sept.
Still sticking to the same old routine. First thing I work on Iphigenie and I hope you'll be pleased with the way she has matured under

these skies, where all day you don't have to give a thought to your body but life is just completely comfortable. Yesterday I went off to the *Campo Marzo* with the play in my pocket and saw on the hillside opposite a couple of nice subjects, I did a quick sketch of them on the blank front and back pages of the MS and I enclose them with this. It would be easy to do a hundred, a thousand such pictures and sketches here in the span of a single hour, I just mustn't let myself get sidetracked into doing it.

Today I saw the *Villa Valmarana* which Tiepolo* decorated and gave free rein to all his virtues and failings. His high style isn't as good as his natural manner, of which there are exquisite examples here, but altogether as decorative art goes it has a very happy touch.

As for architecture, I'm still just going round buildings with my home-made yardstick and that gets me a good way, of course I have a lot to learn, still we'll make do and keep collecting impressions. The main thing is that all these objects that have been working on my imagination for more than thirty years without my ever seeing them, and so were too elevated, are now being toned down into the *easy* feel of *homely* coexistence.

I live very frugally and calmly so that when I see things I'm not in an elevated mood but the things have to do the elevating. That makes you much less prone to error than in the other case. And then I enjoy writing to you, as I enjoy talking to you with the objects before my eyes and sending my distant beloved all the things I hope to tell her about when she's no longer distant. Then it's also a cheering thought that you may have what I'm writing now and more besides in at most six weeks.

But whatever else happens, one needs to see and see again so as to get a pure impression of them. It's a strange thing about first impressions, they're always an extreme mixture of truth and falsehood, I still can't quite work out what goes on.

I'm sad to see the dismal skies over the Tyrolean mountains all the time, you're probably getting bad weather, here it sometimes rains but is then fine again. Mornings and evenings are cool.

25 Sept. Evening 22 hours, 5 o'clock by our time. About Vicenza again. I'm sorry to be leaving this place, there's a lot for me here. If only it were possible to spend some time in this region with you! But we're eternally banished from it; if one wanted to live

here, it would be necessary to become Catholic straight away, so as to get really involved in the people's way of life. Everything invites you to do that, and they're all very easygoing and open.

I was in the library to see the bust of the celebrated jurist Bartolius,* it's in marble in a commanding position. He has a firm, free, honest, handsome face with a fine bone-structure and I'm glad his image too is now in my possession. At the Dominican monastery they have an ancient statue they call Iphigenia. But it's exactly the idea of the vestal virgins, of which we have a small and a large cast. Because the hands are pressed to her sides and wrapped in her garment, these statues have suffered less, but the head is new and much too big.

I've seen a few more buildings and my eye is starting to be well trained, I now have the courage to tackle the mechanical aspects of the art. What I'm pleased about is that none of my old basic ideas are shifting and changing, everything is just getting more clearly defined, developing, and growing to meet me.

I went up the hill of the *Madonna* again. The collection of one of the Servite fathers has lots of items but not a lot of interest. The balcony of the room, though, has a view that you can only look at in dumb amazement. And on a higher floor, from the so-called *foresteria** where they entertain distinguished visitors the view stretches even further, you can see Vicenza too and the mountains of Tyrol.

As you're coming down again, you have a hill to your left, a bit of a peak and standing free, with vines growing all the way to the summit, there are a few large trellises too and at the top to round it off a troop of cypresses. I've been looking at it with constant delight all this last week.

Incidentally, I still like the people of Vicenza a lot; they have a kind of easygoing humanity that comes from living their lives all the time in public. And it's one thing after the other, churches, market, promenading, pilgrimage (that's what I call the walk out to the Virgin), theatre, public spectacles, carnival, etc., and the female sex is mostly good-looking, they are very straightforward with no coquetry and are extremely neatly dressed. I took a good look at them all, and in the whole week didn't see more than one of whom I could confidently say that she was offering her charms for sale.

The men too I find polite and helpful. I go into a bookshop and ask the bookseller for something he doesn't just recall, there are various persons of some rank sitting around, clergy and laypeople. Immediately one of them starts talking to the bookseller, helping him and me with the problem, straight off and without more ado as if we'd known each other for ages.

I've noticed this about them. They look you over from head to foot and seem to have a sharp eye for the detail of your clothes. Now, I take pleasure in wearing these misleading stockings, after which they can't possibly take me for a *gentleman*.* Meanwhile my conduct towards them is very open, courteous, sedate, and I enjoy being able to go about freely and without fear of being recognized. I wonder how long that will last.

I can't tell you how much I've gained in humanity in this short time. But how I also feel what miserable lonely people we must be in the small sovereign states,* because—especially in my position—you can hardly talk to anyone without them wanting something or having some axe to grind. I've never felt the value of sociability so keenly, and the pleasurable anticipation of seeing my far-off friends again.

The buildings I've looked at and walked round again and again.

Looking at the picture of the Adoration of the Magi in the Dominican church, I amused myself with the innocent albeit not orthodoxly sublime thought that the Infant Jesus is scared of the old man who is kneeling and worshipping him, he's pulling a frightened little face.

You get so sick of churches and altarpieces that it's easy to overlook some good things—and I'm only at the start of it.

Here's an observation about something many travellers get wrong, I have myself too on previous journeys.

Anyone who's travelling really thinks he's going to *enjoy* himself for his money. He doesn't expect the things he's heard so much about to be just as heaven and circumstances dictate, he thinks they'll all be as pure* as they are in his imagination, and he finds hardly anything is like that, there's hardly anything he can enjoy in that way. One thing has been destroyed, the next has got stained, one place stinks, another place is thick with smoke, somewhere else is dirty, whether it's the inns or the people, or whatever.

The pleasure from a journey, if you really want it in pure form, is of an abstract kind, I have to discount the discomforts, the repellent aspects, anything that's wrong with my mood or that I don't expect, and seek out in works of art only the artist's idea, its first execution, the life of the original moment when the work was created, and think of it to myself as pure and isolated from all that the universal conditions of time and mutability have done to it. Then I get a pure and lasting enjoyment, and that's what I've travelled for, not for the sake of fleeting moments of fun and relaxation. Exactly the same applies to the contemplation and enjoyment of nature. But when things do all come together and fit, then it's a great bounty, I've had moments like that.

I write to you like this just as things occur to me because I know it will give you pleasure. It can all be said better and more precisely later. All my feelings are for and with you and my dearest hope is to see you again.

Padua, 26th, evening
You can always think of me writing to you as night falls, for by then my day's work is done.

It took me four hours to get across here this morning from Vicenza. As usual with my whole existence packed on to a small, one-seat chaise (*sediola*). Normally you can do it comfortably in three and a half hours, but as I was happy to enjoy the wonderful day in the open air, I was glad the vetturino* was behind schedule. The road goes south-east through the most beautiful plain, you don't have much of a view because it's all between hedges and trees. Till finally you see on your right the beautiful Este hills,* a volcanic chain that runs north–south.

On the way I only wished I could show you at a single glance the profusion of plants that hang down over walls, hedges, trees. The pumpkins on the roofs, etc.

Well, so now I'm in Padua! and in five hours I've seen most of what Volkmann tells you to see; nothing that gave me any real deep satisfaction, but a few things it's good to have seen.

This time I'll follow the order in Volkmann, which you can find in Part 3 on page 638. I'll assume you read the articles, and will just add my notes.

p. 639 *terrible earthquakes*. Perhaps it's through being so near to the Este hills, they're only 6 Italian miles from here, and there are warm springs as you come this way. There may still have been some wicked old remnants hiding in the intestines or rather under the skin of old Mother Earth, although I don't yet have any proper idea of them.

Neighbouring hills. None nearer than the Estes. The town is splendidly situated, I saw it from the Observatorio. Northwards the Tyrolean mountains under snow and half hidden in cloud, and they're joined to the north-west by the volcanic mountains near Vicenza and finally to the west by the nearer Este hills, whose shape and moulding you can plainly see. To the south and west, it's one sea of green without a trace of high ground, tree after tree, bush after bush, plantation after plantation right to the furthest horizon and against the green, countless white houses, villas, churches, etc.

From the Observatorio I could plainly see the tower of St Mark's in Venice and the other lesser towers through my telescope.

p. 641. *The town paving* etc. is lava from the Este hills, I brought some with me.

red marble, a fairly firm red limestone like the Veronese sort.

p. 642 *Maria by Giotto** I couldn't find.

Sacristy was shut.

p. 642. *St Antonio*. I'll tell you about this barbaric building when I'm back.

p. 646. *Cardinal Bembo*. It's a good thing they built churches to the saints; at least then they also have a good place to set up images of rational and noble human beings. He has a handsome face, so to speak forcibly drawn in, and a massive beard. His bust stands between two Ionian columns which look to me to be imitated from the monument to Porto in Vicenza (see p. 677). The inscription is excellent:

> *Petri Bembo Card. imaginem*
> *Hier. Guirinus Ismeni F.*
> *in publico ponendam curavit*
> *ut cujus Ingenii*
> *monumenta aeterna sint*
> *ejus corporis quoque memoria*
> *ne a posteritate desideretur.**

A worthy inscription for the man who was reluctant to read the Bible so as not to ruin his Latin style, and probably his imagination too.*

p. 647. *Helena Cornara*. Well formed not charming, as befits a woman dedicated to Minerva.*

p. 644. *St Agatha by Tiepolo*. The face not sublime yet astoundingly true, physical pain and serenity in suffering beautifully expressed. If only martyrdoms didn't always have to drag with them a crew with those wretched hangdog expressions.

p. 647. *Beheading of John the Baptist by Piazetta.** A really fine picture. Always supposing you like the master's manner. John is kneeling with his hands together in front of him and his right knee against a stone, he's looking up to heaven, a soldier who has tied him up has gone round on his right side and is peering into his face as if he's astonished at the resignation with which the man is facing his fate, higher up there's another soldier who's going to strike the blow but doesn't have the sword, he only holds his arms above him as if he's practising, a man further down is unsheathing the sword. The idea is new and the composition is striking, a hangdog entourage again of course.

p. 648. *Scuola del Santo.* Titian's pictures, marvellous how close they get to the old German Holbein manner. From which nobody on our side of the Alps has recovered. There's an astounding, infinitely promising truth in them. They've given me much food for thought, as indeed a lot of the old pictures have.

p. 649. *Martyrdom of St Justina by Paul Veronese.* He has the flaw I already noticed in Vicenza of putting too many figures into the picture and making them too small. As they look down from such a high altar, they have no *presence.* Everything else is in Volkmann.

650. *In the Abbot's room.* A fine picture by *Quercin da Cento,** Justice and Peace.

ibid. Exquisite book-collection. Undeniably. Ancient writers, the Italian poets. Church fathers, as you'd expect, etc. At a quick glance, it was all good and useful stuff.

ibid. Prato della Valle. All round the square they've put up statues of their famous men and also allowed private persons to erect a statue to some meritorious man from their family, as the inscriptions show. The fair that's held here is famous.

p. 655. *Descent from the Cross* by Bassano.* Well done, and as nobly as it was possible to do such a subject.*

ibid. Salone. If you haven't seen something like this you don't believe it or couldn't imagine it.*

p. 658. *il Bo** I'm glad I didn't have to study there. Again, you couldn't imagine the *constricting feel* of this academic institution if you haven't seen it, particularly the Anatomy Theatre can only be regarded as a miracle. It's beyond all describing.

The Botanical Garden is all the nicer and more cheerful, though not at its best in this season. I shall give the greater part of tomorrow to it. Just walking through it today I learnt a lot.

Goodnight for today! I've scribbled what I could so as to get at least something down on paper.

Padua 27th noon

Today I caught up with some more things. I'd been driven out of the Botanical Garden by rain. I've seen some beautiful things there and pressed some items for you for fun. They grow a lot of exotic plants in this country, up walls or sheltered by them, and then towards the end of October they cover the whole lot and heat it for the few winter months.

Evening, 27 Sept.

As usual, my dear, when the *Ave Maria della Sera* is said my thoughts turn to you; though I mustn't say that, for they're with you all day. Oh if only we appreciated what we have in each other when we're together.

Another thing I did today was to buy Palladio's works in a folio volume. Not the first edition, it's true, but a very careful reprint done by an Englishman.* You have to give it to the English, they've had an appreciation of good things for a long time. And they have a stylish way of showing their good taste.

Today I looked at all the statues in the square again, they were mostly put there by private individuals and guilds, and some foreigners too. For instance the King of Sweden had a statue put up to Gustavus Adolphus because they say he once went to a lecture in Padua. The Archduke Leopold put up statues to Petrarch and Galileo, etc. The statues are done in a modern, straightforward style. They're mostly not too mannered, some are really natural. I also very much like the inscriptions, they're in Latin and there's not a tasteless or petty one among them. There are Popes and Doges at the entrance. It can become a really beautiful square if they remove the wooden *Fiera* and build a stone one on the far side of the square as they apparently plan to do.

This evening I went to St Justina's, which is admittedly not a great church for style, but large and simple, and sat in a corner thinking. I felt very alone, for not a soul in the world who might have thought of me at that moment would have looked for me in this corner.

The city is big and not overpopulated, even more empty now because it's the university vacation and the nobles are living out in the country. So you have to fall back on the ancestral figures on the Prato del Valle.

Once again I've had my botanical ideas splendidly confirmed. It will certainly come and I'm advancing even further. Only it's odd and sometimes it makes me afraid, that such an immense amount is as if pressing in on me that I can't fend off, so that my existence is growing like a snowball, and sometimes it feels like my head can't grasp it or stand it, and yet it's all developing from within, and I can't live if that doesn't happen.

In the Minimite Church I've seen pictures by Mantegna,* one of the older masters, that I'm amazed by! Words can't express the clear, confident present those pictures contain. This whole, true (not just illusory, not mendaciously effect-seeking, not playing on the imagination) this rough, pure, luminous, detailed, conscientious, delicate, circumscribed present which at the same time had something austere, diligent, laborious about it, is what his successors started from, as I saw in pictures of Titian's yesterday, and their intellectual vitality and natural energy, plus the inspiration of the ancients, enabled them to go higher and higher, to raise themselves from the earth and produce heavenly yet true figures. That is the history of art and of every one of the individual great artists after the dark ages.

Architecture still feels infinitely remote, it's odd how everything about it is so alien, so distant, without being new to me.* But I hope that this time I will at least be admitted to its forecourts too.

Now I'm just about packed up here once more, and tomorrow morning I travel on by boat down the Brenta. Today it's been raining, now it's brightened up again and I hope to get my first sight of the Lagoons and the once triumphant bride of the sea at a good time of day and to greet you from her bosom. Now goodnight.

FOURTH SECTION

VENICE

1786

Thus then it was written in the book of destiny that on 28 September, at five by our time, I was to sail out of the Brenta into the Lagoons and see Venice for the first time, and soon afterwards set foot on and reside in the wondrous island city, this Beaver Republic. And so thank God *Venice* is no longer a mere word for me, a name by which so often, as a sworn enemy of empty words, so often I have been affrighted.

As the first gondola came alongside our boat, I suddenly remembered my first childhood toy, which I had not thought of for perhaps twenty years. My father had brought back a beautiful model gondola from Venice, he set great store by it and it was a great thing when I was allowed to play with it. The first tin prows and black cabins of the gondolas, I greeted them all like old acquaintances, like a long-lost early memory.

And as I feel I am only travelling in order to report back to you, now it's night I settle down to tell you all sorts of things.

I'm comfortably put up in the *Queen of England*, not far from St Mark's Square, the greatest advantage of my lodging.

My windows look out on a narrow canal, between two high houses, immediately beneath me is a bridge and opposite is a narrow alley thronged with people. That's where I'm living and that's where I'll stay for a while until I've got my packet for Germany ready and sucked my fill of the image of this city.

The solitude I've so often yearned and sighed for I can enjoy here, if enjoyment it is, for nowhere can you feel so alone as in a milling crowd like this, where you're not known, in Venice there's perhaps hardly a single person who knows me, and I'm not likely to meet him. We had marvellous weather for the trip down here on the Brenta, which is quite well described in Volkmann p. 636, I travelled with the public boat and can't sufficiently praise the propriety and order of such a mixed middle-class society as we had on board. There were a number of really pretty and agreeable women and girls among them. I find it amazingly easy getting along with this people. Just before our boat reached Venice I took a gondola with another passenger and we made our entry. It is a grand and impressive sight.

I hurried to St Mark's Square, and now my mind is the richer and broader for this image too. This evening I'll say no more. I'll find time here to communicate my thoughts to you. Farewell! I love you always with the same heartfelt tenderness.

                                                                29th, morning
Yesterday evening it clouded over completely, I was worried rain was on the way, the seabirds were another sign. Today the weather's magnificent again. Have done my stint on Iphigenie and now I'm dressing and going out. Before I do, hallo and good-morning.

                                                        St Michael's day, evening
At the end of a happy and well-spent day it's always an inexpressibly sweet sensation to sit down and write to you. I was sorry to have to tear myself away from St Mark's Square when night fell; but the fear of getting too far behind with writing drove me back home.

About Venice everything that can be said has been said and printed, so only a few words about the way it comes to meet me. The main thing that stands out is again the idea of *the people*. Great mass! and a necessary, spontaneous form of life. This race didn't flee to these islands for fun, it was no arbitrary force that drove others to unite with them, it was luck that made their situation so favourable, it was luck that they were shrewd at a time when the whole of the northern world still lay caught up in its nonsense, the way these people multiplied and grew wealthier was a necessary consequence. Then they pressed tighter and tighter together, sand and swamp became rock beneath their feet, their houses rose for air like trees growing close together, they had to try for height so as to make up for what they couldn't get in breadth, miserly about every inch of ground and from the start pressed into narrow spaces, they didn't allow more width for alleyways than would just divide house from house and let people pass, and anyway water was street, square, promenade for them, in short Venetians had to become a new kind of creature and so Venice too can only be compared with itself. Just as no other street in the world can compare with the Grand *Canal*, so too there is nothing to compete with the space in front of St Mark's Square. I mean the great stretch of water that is embraced on one side by the half-moon of Venice proper, with the island of San Giorgio facing, a bit further to the right the Giudecca and its canal, and further right still the Doge's Palace and the mouth of the Grand Canal. I'll enclose a map of Venice and make things quite clear by drawing in the lines of sight to the main things that strike the eye when you come out between the two columns of St Mark's Square. (NB In the end I haven't, because it really doesn't give a proper idea.)

I've contemplated it all with a calm attentive eye and taken delight in this great life-form. After eating I went out on foot to begin with so as to take things gradually, and noting only the compass directions plunged without a guide into the labyrinth of the city. You can't imagine that either, without you've seen it. Usually you can span the width of the alleyways with outstretched arms, or almost, in the smaller alleys you couldn't even stretch your arms right out. There are broader streets, but they're all narrow in proportion. I easily found the Grand Canal and the Rialto Bridge. It's a grand beautiful sight, especially looking down from the bridge, as it's arched and rises quite high. The canal is thick with ships and teeming with gondolas, particularly today because on the Feast of St Michael the well-dressed women were all making their pilgrimage to church, and at least had themselves ferried across. I met some very beautiful beings.

When I was tired I took a gondola, left the narrow alleys behind, and went right through the Canal Grande, round St Clara's Island, along the great lagoon, into the Giudecca Canal as far as St Mark's Square, and was now suddenly one more Lord of the Adriatic, as every Venetian feels himself to be when he reclines in his gondola. I honoured the memory of my poor father whose greatest pleasure was to recount these things. It is a great work of collective human effort worthy of all respect, a splendid monument not to a *ruler* but to a *people*, and if their lagoons are gradually filling up and stinking and their trade is getting weaker and their power has declined, that doesn't make their republic any less venerable to me in its whole conception and essence. It is subject to time like everything else in the world of phenomena.

We'll be able to talk endlessly about this, including things you're not supposed to talk about here, like the state and its secrets, which I think I know well enough without anybody having to give them away.

Now a few observations with Part 3 of Volkmann as a guide.

p. 509. St Mark's you must look at an engraving of. The architecture is worthy of any nonsense that may ever have been taught or practised in it. I always frivolously think of the façade as a colossal crab. At least I reckon I could design an enormous crustacean with these proportions.

p. 513. *Ancient horses** These exquisite animals stand here like sheep that have lost their shepherd. When they stood closer together on a more worthy building, in front of the triumphal chariot of a world-conqueror, it may have been a noble sight. Still, thank God that Christian enthusiasm hasn't melted them down and made chandeliers and crucifixes out of them. May they stand here in honour of St Mark, since we owe their preservation to St Mark.

p. 515. *The Doge's Palace*, especially the façade looking on to St Mark's Square. The strangest thing that I think the human mind has produced. More when we meet. I have a notion, I won't put it higher than that. It's that the first practitioners of the architectural art imitated the ruins of Antiquity when they were still half-buried and the spirit of their successors has now cleared away the rubble and brought out the beauty of the form.

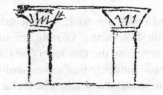

When you see columns like these, don't you feel that part is still buried in the earth, and yet the lower colonnade of the Doge's Palace has these dimensions.

p. 528. Columns on the Piazzetta.

Both of granite, the one with a height probably 10 times its diameter is of red granite whose polish and colour has been preserved, it's so slender and delightful you can't tear your eyes away from it.

The other is about 8 diameters high, so may belong to the Doric order as the first one does to the Composite, it's of white granite that has suffered at the hands of time and developed a kind of shell, about as thick as the back of a biggish knife-blade, which has turned matt and is now peeling off in some places. On the Piazzetta side of St Mark's there are two smaller columns of exactly this kind of stone where you notice the same thing happening.

Apart from St Mark's I haven't been into any buildings. There's enough to do outside, and the people are endlessly interesting. I spent a long time at the fish-market today and watched the way they haggle and bargain with extraordinary intensity, alertness, and shrewdness.

It's also great fun watching the public goings-on of their legal practices. The notaries and the rest sit there each at his desk writing away, somebody comes up to him to ask him to do a document, etc. Others are walking about and so forth. It's a constant communal life and what a necessary part of this tableau the beggars are. Without them we wouldn't have the *Odyssey* or the Story of Dives and Lazarus.* I'm making a terrible mess again, but I can't wait to get the words down on the paper.

30th, evening

When life begins for the Venetians, I withdraw and go home to talk to you a bit. Even the maid asked me yesterday why I don't like to go out in the evening.

Today I've been slowly extending my idea of Venice again. I now have the plan of the city, then I went up the tower of St Mark's, where your eye is met by what must surely be a unique spectacle. It was midday and bright sunshine so that I could make out everything near and far without an eyeglass. The tide was in over the lagoons.

p. 532. Across the *lido*, a narrow strip of ground that closes off the lagoons, I saw the sea and some sails on it for the first time. There are galleys and frigates anchored in the lagoons, meant to be joining Admiral Emo,* but the wind is in the wrong quarter.

The hills near Padua and Vicenza and the Tyrolean Alps frame the picture to the west and north quite wonderfully.

Towards evening I got lost without a guide again in the most remote quarters of the city and tried to find my way out of this labyrinth without asking directions. You find where you are in the end, but it's an incredible tangle, and mine is the best way to really persuade your senses that is so, on top of which I've been noting down to the last detail the behaviour, way of life, customs, and nature of the inhabitants. Dear Lord, what a poor good animal man is.

The quays make a pleasant walk.

The three days I've been here, I've seen a fellow telling stories to a more-or-less large audience. I can't understand a word. But nobody laughs, sometimes the listeners smile—they, as you can imagine, are from the very lowest class. And he has nothing striking or ludicrous in his manner, rather a certain sober look and a variety and precision in his movements which I only noticed this evening. I must take a closer look at him.

Next Monday the *Opera Buffa* and two comic theatres are opening. So we're going to give ourselves a treat too. I hope it will turn out better than in Vicenza. Otherwise there isn't much to report today. Apart from some hard work on Iphigenie, I've spent most of my time on Palladio, and can't put him down. My good angel made me pursue the book that I wanted Jagemann* to send for four years ago, but he got me the more recent edition of the Works. And yet, again! what use would they have been to me if I hadn't seen his buildings? In Verona and Vicenza I saw what I could for myself, it was only in Padua I found the book, now I'm studying it and the scales are falling from my eyes, the mists are dissolving and I understand the objects I see. Simply as a book it's a great work. And what a man he was! My love, how happy it makes me that I've devoted my life to what is true, as it's now such an easy transition to greatness, which is the highest purest point of truth.

The revolution that I foresaw and that is now going on within me is the same as has happened to every artist who for a long time was diligently true to nature and now beheld the remains of the great ancient spirit, his soul swelled within him and he felt a kind of inward transfiguration of himself, a feeling of freer life, higher existence, lightness and grace.

I wish to God I could keep my Iphigenie another half-year, people would be able to sense the southern climate in her even more.

1 October, evening 8 o'clock

I'm coming to you later than usual today, yet will have a great deal to say. This morning I worked at Iphigenie for a long time and it went on well. No two days are alike and I'm surprised I manage so well in this foreign life, but it's a sign that I'm still in firm possession of myself. Then I went to the Rialto and St Mark's Square. Since I learned that Palladio made a design for a bridge over to the Square, and since I've seen him in his works, perhaps I'm allowed a few niggles about the Rialto as it now is. I'll expand on that when we meet. Then I went through several quarters of the city to get to the Square and, as it happened to be Sunday, I did some thinking about how dirty Venice is. The authorities do make some provision. People sweep the muck into nooks and corners, I see big boats plying back and forth, and in some places putting in, to transport the sweepings, which people from the surrounding islands use as manure. But it really is inexcusable that the city isn't cleaner, since it's really designed to be clean, all the streets have an even surface, and even in the remote quarters they at least have a raised brick edge, where necessary there's a bit of a camber in the middle, and depressions at the sides to catch the water and carry it away into underground channels. Some further basic measures would make it infinitely easier to turn Venice into the cleanest of cities, as she is the most bizarre. I couldn't refrain from making a plan for it as I went along.

After dinner I studied more Palladio, who makes me very happy, and then went out with the map of the city in my hand looking for the Church of the *Mendicanti*, which I duly found all right.

The women were performing an oratorio behind the grating, as usual the church was full of people listening. The music very beautiful, and magnificent voices. An alto sang King Saul, not the voice I was expecting. Some passages in the music were infinitely beautiful, I enclose the text, it's such Italian Latin that in many places you can't help laughing; but plenty of scope for the music. It would have been a real delight if the wretched conductor hadn't beaten time by slapping a rolled up score against the grating in a quite disgraceful way, as if he was dealing with schoolboys who needed teaching, and they'd done the piece often, it was absolutely unnecessary and ruined the whole impression, much as if a beautiful statue were set up with bits of scarlet rag stuck on all the joints.* The intrusive sound undoes any harmony, and this is a musician and he can't hear it, or rather he wants the slapping to draw attention to his presence, whereas it would be better if he let the audience guess at his quality from the perfection of the performance. I know the French do things that way, I wouldn't have expected it of the Italians. And the audience seems used to it.

I had some thoughts about that too, and will communicate them if I find them further confirmed.

Tomorrow I'm going to begin looking at things closely. I'm now familiar with the whole layout, there's no risk of being confused by the detail, and I'll take a firm image of Venice away with me. Today for the first time I was accosted by a prostitute in broad daylight in an alley near the Rialto.

This evening there was a splendid moon. A storm came up over the sea from the south-east, that is from the Dalmatian mountains, there was lightning, the storm passed over the moon, broke up, and went on towards the Tyrolean Alps, so that's the same wind that throws all the clouds that have formed further south against the German mountains and perhaps means trouble for you in the north. Still, I have hopes for you, as the mountains are mostly clear.

I've done some quick sketches on grey paper of the way things looked over the water this evening.

Farewell. I do feel tired in the evenings. I'm sure you'll sometimes take the wish for the deed, even if I don't manage to say anything very clever.

2 October, evening

A word before I go to the opera.

p. 569. St *Giorgio* a fine monument to Palladio, although in this case he was following not so much his own genius as the genius of place.

p. 566. *Carità*.* I found an indication in Palladio's Works that what he intended here was a building to imitate the private dwellings of Antiquity, the upper classes naturally. I hurried off there avid to see it but alas hardly a tenth of it is executed. Yet even this part worthy of his divine genius. A perfection in the design and a meticulousness in the execution such as I hadn't previously come across. In the mechanical aspects too, as the greater part was put up in brick (of which it's true I've seen other examples) a fine precision. I did some drawing after Palladio today and want to assimilate him at the deepest level.

p. 530. Library, rather the hall of antiquities that you go through first, precious things. A robe of a Minerva, a Cleopatra; I say 'robe', because I mentally break off the restored heads and arms straight away. A Ganymede supposed to be by Phidias* and a celebrated Leda. Again just fragments, the first well restored, the second moderately, but with a strong feeling of sensuality.

I can't forget the Carità. He also added a staircase to it that he praises himself and which really is very beautiful.

3 October

Yesterday evening opera at *St Moisé*. Nothing really enjoyable about it. The text, the music, the players all lacked the inner energy needed to raise things to the highest level. It was all not bad, but only the two women took any trouble, not just to act well but to *project* themselves and *please*. Well, that's something. They have good figures, good voices, suitably lively and pleasing. On the other hand, none of the men had any of the inner power and zest to make much impression on the audience. And no positively brilliant voice.

The ballet miserably uninventive, and duly whistled off the stage. A few splendid leapers, the women taking great care to show the audience all their best parts.

Today though I saw a quite different comedy, which was more enjoyable. I was at a court hearing in the Doge's Palace.

It was an important case and was even being heard, fortunately for me, in the vacation.

One of the lawyers who spoke was everything that a *Buffo caricato** should be. Figure: fat, short, but agile. A tremendously prominent profile. A voice like brass and vehement, as if everything he said was in deep and deadly earnest. I call it a comedy because it's probably all set up in advance before the production is put on for the public and the judges too know in advance what they're going to decide. Even so, this way of doing things is immensely preferable to the hole-and-cornerism of our chanceries. I'll tell you the full circumstances and how agreeably without pomp, how natural it all is, when we meet.

Evening

Seen a lot. Just a few words as a reminder

p. 565. *I Scalzi*, marble enough, and not at all badly put together; but nothing of the elevated spirit that can only be sensed in inimitable measure, order, harmony.

566. *La Salute* the middle vessel on which the cathedral rests is of

a height and breadth that are not to be scorned. But the whole in every detail is just one example of bad taste after another, a church that is worthy to have miracles happen in it.

567. Marriage-feast at Cana. A picture well known from engravings, and charming enough in that form. Magnificent women's heads and the tasteless subject of a long table with guests very nobly handled. The ceiling decorations by Titian a very crazy choice of subjects for a ceiling; yet beautiful and splendidly executed.

Isaac's father has him by the forelock, the rest of his hair hangs down and he's looking down in a graceful posture. David, having killed Goliath, puts his hands together in a free and easy gesture as he looks up to heaven.

p. 577. *Il Redentore*. A beautiful and grandiose work of Palladio's. The façade much more praiseworthy than the one on *St Giorgio*. These are works that have been engraved, we can talk about them. Just one general word. *Palladio* had absorbed so much of the existence of the ancients and felt the littleness and narrowness of the time into which he'd been born, like a great man who won't resign himself but sets out as far as possible to reshape the rest to his own noble conceptions. Thus he was not happy, so I infer from a mild phrase in his book, with the way people went on building Christian churches in the old basilica form, he tried to make his churches more like ancient temples. That led to some features that don't quite fit, which I think he managed to integrate in the case of *St Redentore*, but are too obtrusive in *St Giorgio*. Volkmann says a bit about this but doesn't hit the nail on the head.

St Redentore is exquisite inside as well. Everything is by Palladio, including the altar designs. Only the niches, which he meant to be filled with statues, have garish painted wooden figures.

In honour of St Francis, the *Capuchin fathers* had given a side-altar the full decorative treatment. You couldn't see anything of the stonework except the Corinthian capitals. All the rest seemed to be covered over with a splendid tasteful embroidery in arabesque style, the nicest of its kind I've seen. I was especially surprised at the broad gold-embroidered foliage and tendrils. I looked closer and found it was a very nice piece of *trompe-l'œil*. What I'd taken for gold was pressed straw stuck on paper in lovely patterns and the background painted with vivid colours, and that so variegated and attractive that this jest, which in material terms was not worth a penny, and which probably some of them had done themselves for free, would have cost thousands if it had been genuine. We can do it some time. A fault in the whitewashing and painting of churches I note just as a reminder.

573. *Gesuati*, a true Jesuit church. Cheerful paintings by Tiepolo. In the ceiling pieces some of the charming female saints are showing more than their calves, if my eyeglass doesn't deceive me. The picture Volkmann quotes is a foolish subject, but very nicely executed.

I ought to say more about the Doge's Palace, which I saw this morning. Maybe tomorrow. As you can see, I'm just shooting everything on the wing. But it's caught for good in the perceptions of eye and heart.

4 October, noon

Today it rained and I made use of the time and got straight down to work on Iphigenie. Now a few words for my beloved.

Yesterday I went to the comedy at the *Teatro S. Luca*, which was a real pleasure, extemporized, performed in masks and with great naturalness, energy, and competence. The standard isn't all of a piece. Pantaloon is very good and one of the women, who looks very like Countess Lanthieri, no great actress but speaks excellently and knows how to carry herself. A crazy plot with incredible twists and turns that provided a good three hours' entertainment. But it's the *people* every time who are the basis on which it all rests. It's the whole that does it, not the parts. In the square and on the quays and in the gondolas and in the palace. The buyer and the seller, the beggar and the seaman, the lawyer and his adversary—all living and active and involved and talking and asserting and shouting and making offers and singing and scolding and cursing and making a din. And in the evening they go to the theatre and see and hear their daily life, only artfully put together, more charmingly tricked out with a bit of fantasy woven in, etc. and they take a childlike pleasure and shout some more and clap and make a din. From one night to the next, from midnight to midnight it all goes on in exactly the same way.

I scarcely think I've seen more natural acting than these masks, really an outstanding natural talent.

As I write this there's noise on the canal beneath my window that lasts beyond midnight. For better and worse they're always up to something between them.

The Farsetti house has a precious collection of casts of the best pieces from Antiquity. I'll say nothing about the ones I already knew from Mannheim* and elsewhere, and mention only new acquaintances: the Cleopatra colossal in repose, she has attached the asp to her arm and is entering the sleep of death. The mother Niobe covering her youngest daughter with her cloak to protect her from Apollo's arrows, several gladiators, an Amor resting wrapped in his wings, a seated and a standing Marius, they're works that can give delight for thousands of years and it still won't exhaust the value of the artist. Also some very fine busts. I just feel even now how far behind I am in my knowledge of these things, still, it will come with a rush, at least I know the way. Palladio has shown me the way to this and to all of art and all of life. That perhaps sounds a bit odd, but yet it's not as paradoxical as when the sight of a pewter dish gave Jacob Böhme illumination about the whole universe.*

If I come back and you are still nice to me, you shall know all about my secrets too.

Another thing in this collection is a cast of the frieze and the cornice of the Temple of Antoninus and Faustina whose outlines I'll trace lightly from the Palladio edition, to give you a quick idea. Although no drawing can match the architectural presence that springs out at you. This is only a miserable little picture anyway (I've left it out, it was useless).

Tomorrow, Thursday, the *St Luca* troupe are playing again, according to the advertisements a kind of historical play. Saturday is solemn mass at St Justina with the Doge there, whom I shall see then in full ceremonial fig along with the nobility. Sunday is the consecration of St Mark's where he'll appear again too. Till then we'll see what there is for us still to see in Iphigenie and the Venetian sights.

p. 523. Paradise by Tintoretto. Another glorification of the Mother of God. But in spirit doesn't come near the one in the *Casa Bevi l'aqua* at Verona. One thing I think I've noticed is that Tintoretto does small figures better than big ones. With the small ones he could give free rein to his natural grace and lightness of touch, and the larger scale was a hindrance.

In this Paradise too there are larger figures and the picture is still by him, but that luminosity of spirit has vanished. He also painted the Verona piece when he was still young, as I conclude from all the signs and the provocative Eve, this picture in old age. Eve is quite hidden.

All the rest of the paintings in the Palace I've seen and had explained to me, and at least I have a mental image of the whole and of the most remarkable subjects.

I've now hired a servant. A splendid old man. A German—who every day saves me what he costs. He's been right through Italy as companion to people of rank and knows his way around. He keeps the Italians in check as is needed. For example, he gives the exactly right least tip in each place, I have to pass as a merchant everywhere.

He had a set-to with a gondolier over 10 soldi, it made a tremendous row, and the gondolier was right at that. But he takes no notice, he did much the same today in the Arsenal. He reminds me a bit of Wende,* has his manners too. I was glad to be by myself the first days, and I'm glad that I have him now.

I had a fancy to get myself a tabarro* and all the trappings, for people are already going about in masks. But when I thought about it it seemed too expensive, and am I not enough of a carnival mask for them as I am? I'll buy myself a Vitruvius* instead, that's a pleasure will last beyond Venice and the carnival.

Evening

I have a set routine now, when it strikes night-time I go home. The noisy square is too lonely for me, and I need you. Now this and that.

I've now heard the following speak in public:

(1) Three fellows in the square telling stories each in his way.
(2) Two preachers
(3) Two agents
(4) The comic actors, especially Pantaloon.

They all have something in common, both because they're of one nation which is constantly involved in living and talking, and because they imitate each other. They have certain favourite gestures which I must take note of, and in general I practise doing what they do and will tell you stories in this style when I come back, although they lose a lot of their originality in another language, I also enclose the figure

of the lawyer, which is much less of a caricature than the real thing
was.

Today for the feast of St Francis I was in his church, *Francesco alle
vigne*. The loud voice of the Capuchin was accompanied by the
shouts of things being sold outside the church, a kind of antiphonal
effect, I stood halfway between the two and it sounded rather good.
This is another church that Palladio grafted on to an old one, and the
strange contradictions I was talking about yesterday show up again
here. I'm very much looking forward to studying all this more
thoroughly later.

This evening I'm going to the theatre, *St Chrysostomo* where they do comedies translated from the French, I must see what kind of effect that produces.

p. 520. In a room next to the *Sala del Consiglio dei Dieci** which also belongs to this fearsome tribunal there hangs a delightful Dürer opposite a Raphael; when I was looking at the former, one of the *avogadori** came in from the next room, a fantastic figure, a fine sight in his get-up, and my companions bowed almost to the ground. He called someone, was in general quite affable, went just as he had come. They also let me take a peek into the room where the three State Inquisitors meet, so I also know what it looks like in there. I'm glad to see how they keep my Birds in order.

5 October. After dinner

This morning I was at the Arsenal and it was interesting enough for me, as I don't yet know anything about the sea and so here too I had to go back to primary school, so to speak. For certainly everything here has the look of an old family which is still active but where the blossom and the best fruiting time are past.

As I'm also trying to learn something about craftsmen, I saw some remarkable things. I climbed up on the completed frame of an 84-gun vessel. A similar ship, fully built and fitted out, burned down to the waterline six months ago on the *Riva de Sciavoni*. The powder chamber was not very full and when it went up there was no great damage done. The neighbouring houses lost their windowpanes.

I've seen beautiful oak-wood from Istria being worked. I can't say too often how much my hard-won knowledge of natural things, which mankind need as materials and apply for their profit, helps me generally and throws light on matters. For example, my mineralogical and oryctological knowledge* of rocks gives me a head start in architecture.

On this journey I hope and intend to achieve a settled view of the fine arts, really impress their sacred image on my mind, and keep them as a source of private pleasure. But then to turn my attention to craftsmen and when I come back study chemistry and mechanics. For the time of beauty is over, our day demands only what is an urgent and strict necessity.

I already have preliminary thoughts and feelings about the renaissance of the arts in Italy in the Middle Ages, and how this Astraea* soon abandoned Earth again and how the whole picture fits together. How Roman history rises from the past to meet me! A pity, a pity, my love! all a little late. Oh why didn't I have a sensible Englishman as my father, instead of being left to acquire and conquer all this all by myself as I was, and still am.

It's raining and I'm sitting by the fire. When will I pour tea for you again beside mine?

Since I promised you coffee from Alexandria, you probably didn't think I'd even get it in Venice. I've already asked, myself or through people who know, in various places, but I'm not yet confident, I have to be quite sure. The kind I've seen was going to cost a ducat for seven pounds, that wouldn't be bad. Mind you, transport from here to the depths of the continent in Thüringen would add something, but no matter, you shall have some.

Yesterday I didn't go to the comedy as I'd intended. Today I hope to see a tragedy and am very curious what it will be like.

With architecture things are getting better by the day. If you jump in, you learn to swim. I've now got a rational grasp of the orders of columns and can mostly say *why* they're as they are too. I can now keep the dimensions and relationships in my mind, whereas I found them incomprehensible and impossible to retain when they were merely something to be learned by heart.

A word about the *Bucentaur*.* It's a luxury galley. But a fine conception and well executed. I keep coming back to my old principle: if an artist has a genuine subject, he can produce something genuine. The task here was to make a galley that would be worthy to carry the heads of a republic on the most solemn day to the sacrament of their time-honoured overlordship. And it is finely executed. Ornamentation every inch! You can't therefore say it's overloaded with ornament. Nothing but carving and gilding, not for any practical use, a true *monstrance* to show the people their leaders in full magnificence. And we know that the people, just as they like to decorate their own hats, also like to see their rulers magnificent and dressed up. It's a real family heirloom by which you can see what the Venetians were and what they thought of themselves.

The way I'm writing all this down for you, I won't have much left for when I'm back. I can definitely say I haven't had a single thought that seemed to me worth anything without at least giving some hint of it in a few words. As it's not yet time for the theatre, a word about

Palladio following on from yesterday's. In the works he carried out, especially the churches, I've seen a lot to criticize alongside the very greatest things, so that it felt as if he was standing there beside me and saying: this and this I did against my will, but I did it because that was the only way I could get anywhere near my ideal in these circumstances.

It seems to me that when looking at a square, a dimension of height or breadth, a pre-existing church, an older house for which he was supposed to add façades, he simply thought: how are you going to get this whole thing into the grandest form, you may have to botch this or that detail, here or there it will produce an incongruity, but never mind, the whole will have great style and you'll get pleasure from working on it, and so he put up the great picture he had in his mind even in places where it didn't quite fit, where he had to fragment or mutilate it. That's why I so value the wing in the *Carità*, because there he was doing exactly what he wanted. If it were finished, then perhaps there would now be no more perfect piece of architecture in existence in the world.

I'm getting an increasingly clear picture of all this (i.e. the way he thought and the way he worked) as I read more of his works, or rather see how he treats the ancients. For he uses few words, but they are all weighty. It's the fourth book,* on the Temples of Antiquity, that is a real guide to the way you should see Rome.

The really remarkable thing is the way other architects before and after him have chewed over these difficulties and the only solution they've found is a golden mediocrity. I'll grasp all that even better when I've got past the elementary classes.

Night

I've just been laughing all the way home from the tragedy and will tell you about it before I go to sleep. The play wasn't bad. The author had put together all the tricks of the tragic trade and it was grateful material for the actors. Most of the situations were familiar, but some were new and quite ingenious. In the end the only thing left was for the fathers to stab each other, which duly passed off happily. Whereupon the curtain fell, to great applause. But the clapping only got louder, the audience shouted *fuora* and at last the two principal couples condescended to creep out from behind the curtain, bow and scrape, and exit on the other side. But the audience still wasn't satisfied, they kept on clapping and shouting *i morti!* and it went on and on till the two old men came out and bowed, whereupon there were shouts of *bravi i morti!** They got lots of applause and off they went. The joke loses a lot if you don't have the shouts of *bravo! bravi!* that the Italians use all the time ringing in your ears, as I have, and then suddenly you even hear them calling out this compliment to the dead. It had me really chuckling. Good night! *Felicissima notte!** the Italians say.

6 October, morning

Yesterday's tragedy taught me a lot. First, I heard the way the Italians handle and declaim their eleven-syllable iambics. Then I saw how cleverly Gozzi* linked masks with tragic characters. That is the real drama for this people. For they want to be moved in a crude fashion. They don't seem to me to have any tender sympathy with the tragic victim, they just enjoy it if the hero speaks well, for they set a lot of store by good speaking, then they want to have a laugh, or some kind of stage foolery.

It was comical when the tyrant gave his son a sword and demanded he should kill his own wife with it, she being there on stage, the people started to disapprove of this action vociferously, they weren't far off interrupting the play and demanding the old tyrant should take his sword back. Whereupon the whole dramatic development would have been ruined. It really was a silly, unnatural situation too in the circumstances, and the people spotted that at once.

I also now have a better understanding of the long speeches and the way they argue the pros and cons in Greek tragedy. The Athenians were keener still on hearing people speak and even better judges of it than the Italians, and they learned something from the courts where they hung around all day.

Afternoon

This morning I went over with my old guardian spirit *al lido,** a spit of land that closes the lagoons off and divides them from the sea. We got out and walked right across it, I heard a loud noise, it was the sea,* and soon I saw it. It was pounding high against the beach as it withdrew, for it was around noon and the tide starting to ebb. So now that's something else I've seen with my own eyes, and I followed it as it retreated over the lovely threshing-floor it leaves behind. I would have loved to have the children here* with me for the seashells. I picked up enough myself, just like a child, especially as I have a use for them.

People eat a lot of squid here, I got them to give me some of the black liquid and plan to get more yet. I'll let it dry in the shells and send it you, use some of it and keep some for me, I can get as much as I like. The colour is pitch black, mixed with water it's a bit gritty, but add some bister and it will be all right. We must try it and I'll ask around whether there's anything else needs bearing in mind or doing.

On the *lido* not far from the sea there are English graves and further on Jewish ones, they aren't supposed to rest in hallowed ground. I found the grave of the noble consul *Smith* and his first wife, I owe him my copy of Palladio* and thanked him for it over his unhallowed grave.

The sea is a grand sight. I must try to arrange a trip out in a fishing boat.

Evening

I'm really happy and contented since I've had Minerva to accompany and support me* in the figure of the old servant I hired. So precise in everything, so sharp in making economies, I've never seen anything like it. Always the shortest route, always the lowest price, always the best of what we're looking for. If only it fitted my plans to stay on in Venice, even just for three months, so that I could study Venetian history and make a few acquaintances. With my way of seeing things and with this honest spy, I'd reckon to put together a fine mental image of Venice.

By the sea today I found various plants whose similar habit gave me a clue to their characteristics. All of them are simultaneously thick-stemmed and vigorous growers, sappy and tough, and it's obvious that the ancient salt in the sand and even more the salt air makes them this way. They're bursting with juices like water-plants, they're firm, tough like mountain plants. Where their leaf-tips tend to spikes, as with thistles, they're tremendously sharp and strong. I found a bush of leaves like that, I took it for our coltsfoot, but here armed with sharp weapons and the leaf like leather, I pressed some. (*Eryngium maritimum.*)

Similarly the seed-pods, the stems all thick and firm. The rushes sharp and stiff so they really prick you. I found some varieties of sponge and some insect cases washed up on the beach. How satisfying it feels that this is now all world and nature and no longer something in a glass case.

I look forward with pleasure to all the kinds of knowledge that nod to me from this side and that, and I shall gladly return to books.

The fish-market and the many products of the sea give me pleasure, I often go across there and shine a light on the hapless ocean denizens who have been snatched from their element.

This morning I also saw the Doge's chambers where his portrait hangs, a handsome man of benevolent appearance.

Another Titian. Delightful brushwork, but otherwise nothing to enthuse over.

The horses on St Mark's seen near to. Excellent figures! From below I'd just about noticed that they had patches of colour, partly a lovely metal sheen, partly touches of copperish green. Close up you can see they were completely gilded and are covered all over with weals, as the barbarians wouldn't file the gold but tried to hack it off. Never mind, at least that way the shape was left. A magnificent team. I'd love to hear someone who really knows horses talk about them.

What seems to me strange is that up there they look heavier and from down on the square they look as delicate as deer, though it is possible to explain it.

The domes and vaults of St Mark's and their side surfaces are full of coloured figures on a gold ground, all mosaic work. Some are very fine, others not great, according to which master did the design and which artist executed it. It really came home to me how much everything depends on the initial invention, that has to have the right proportions and the true spirit, since working with little square pieces of glass, and here not even in the neatest way, they can equally well follow a good and a bad pattern. This artistic technique, as you know, is now very highly developed.

7 October, morning

Today I haven't been able to produce a single line of Iphigenie, so I'll write to you straight away in order to make good use of my fresh day.

Last night I saw Crébillon's *Electra** at the *St Crisostomo* theatre, in

translation of course. I can't say how tasteless and tedious I found it.
The actors are fair enough and the audience can be fobbed off with
one or two good passages. Orestes alone has three different 'poetic'
narratives in one scene, and in the end he goes mad enough to drive
you mad. The Electra is like Madame Bechtolsheim,* only taller,
more solid, with good carriage, speaks the verse well, only from
beginning to end crazed, as the role required. Still, I again learned
something. The eleven-syllable Italian line creates great problems in
the declaiming, because the final syllable is always short and therefore always rises, whatever the actor declaiming it wants. I've also
been thinking that I'd quite happily put on my Iphigenie with this
troupe and in front of this audience, only I'd change one or two
things, as I would have had to do anyway if I'd been making it
suitable for our theatres and our public at home.

But oh dear. It seems the last spark of my attachment to the
theatre is fated to be put out. You won't believe how empty, how
absolutely null all that feels to me. I'm also beginning to understand
how much of a come-down Euripides* was from the art of his predecessors, and yet he still got an incredible reception. If you have
eyes to see, it's clear how it all came about.

Evening

If I hadn't got you to write to, I wouldn't have come back home yet.
The full moon in a perfect clear sky over the lagoons, the islands, the
strange city, makes a magnificent spectacle, the Square looks like a
bizarre opera setting, and everywhere's packed with people.

Now in order.

This morning I was at the solemn service that the Doge has to
attend in honour of an ancient victory over the Turks.* It was held in
St Justina's.

When the golden barques arrive bearing the Doge and a part of
the nobility, the strangely clad boatmen labour at their red oars, on
the banks the clergy, the Fraternities* stand waiting and jostling,
with their wax tapers carried high on poles and long portable silver
candlesticks, and the long violet robes of the Savii, the ministers of
the Republic, then the long red ones of the Senators enter and finally
the Old Man in his long golden robe with the ermine cape dis-
embarks, three take up his train, and then as many *Nobili* again
follow, all this in front of the church portal, with the Turkish

banners held in front of the door: you suddenly feel you're looking at an ancient embroidered tapestry, but one that's admirably designed.

For a northern fugitive like me this ceremony was a delight. With us, where all solemnities are short-coat occasions and where the biggest ceremonies you can think of are conducted with shouldered arms, this kind of thing wouldn't be right: but for a place like Venice these trailing robes and peaceable enactments *are* right. The Doge is a man of fine stature and appearance. But you can see he's ill and is just about holding up under the heavy robe to maintain the dignity of the occasion, for the rest he looks much like the grandpa of the whole race and is altogether kind and affable.

The costume looks very well. The little flap on his cap doesn't spoil the effect, because it's of a fine transparent stuff and rests on the whitest, lightest hair imaginable.

Some fifty *Nobili* in long dark red robes were with him, mostly fine figures, not one caricature among them. Several of them tall, with large heads, strong profiles, white, soft, without looking bloated or dreadfully sated. Rather they look effortlessly judicious, calmly sure of themselves. Lightness of being, and running through it all a certain gaiety.

When everyone was arrayed in the church and the Mass began, the Fraternities processed in through the main door and out through the side door after receiving man by man, or rather pair by pair, the holy water and bowing to the high altar, the Doge, and the nobility.

I've been to the Pisani Palace. A pity that you sense its republican element so strongly and yet that too is good in a way. Built over time, not fully carried through because of local hindrances, very high, a fine view of the whole of Venice from its roof. Handsome rooms, very habitable too, although not much in the way of decoration, which in any case people didn't know much about in olden times, and anything here is old. (I mean of course the original design.)

I notice a fine kind of flooring that's common here. They do a good imitation of all kinds of granite and porphyry, sometimes with pretty fantastic colours, and the floors are kept clean and sparkling.

Scuola di St Marco. Beautiful pictures by Tintoretto, whom I've always loved and love more and more.

Ballon. As in Verona. There were a couple of excellent players. The onlookers placed bets and had a great time. And the most common man had the right to comment.

This evening I'd ordered the famous boatman performers who sing Tasso and Ariosto* to their own tunes. It was a moonlight night, I took a gondola, one singer in the bow, one in the stern, they began their song and sang the verses turn and turn about. The melody, which we know through Rousseau,* is something between chorale and recitative, it keeps the same movement throughout without having a regular time, the modulation too stays constant, except that in order to match the content of the lyric they use a kind of declamation that changes the tone and the measure.

But this last is really the spirit and the life of it.

How the melody originally came about I won't enquire, enough, it's just what is needed by someone idly modulating something to himself and fitting poems he knows by heart to the tune. With a strong carrying voice (the people are impressed by power more than anything) he sits on the bank of an island, a canal, on a bark, and lets his song ring out as far as he can. And it does carry a long way over the silent surface. Far away someone else hears it who knows the melody, understands the words, and replies with the next lines, the first man replies again in his turn, and thus each of them is the other's echo and the song goes on for nights, entertains them without wearying them. So the further they are apart, the more charming their song is, if the listener is between the two then he's in the best place. So as to let me hear this they got out on the Giudecca quay, spread out along the canal, I walked up and down between them in such a way that I was always leaving the one who was starting to sing and approaching the one who was ceasing. It was only at that point that the sense of the singing dawned on me. And then, as a voice from the distance it sounded strange, like a lament without mourning—and has something incredibly moving, to the point of tears. I put it down to my mood, but my old chap said as we were going home: *è singolare come quel canto intenerisce, e molto più quando è più ben cantato.** He told me you have to hear the lido women singing, particularly the ones from furthest out, *Malamocco* and *Palestrina*, they apparently sing Tasso to this and similar melodies. It's their custom, when their menfolk are fishing out at sea, to sit on the shore in the evening and sing these songs in their carrying voices until they hear the men singing back from far out, so it's a conversation. Don't you think that's lovely? very lovely! It's easy to imagine that someone *listening* close by might take no pleasure in these voices as they struggle with the waves of the ocean. But how human and true the idea behind the singing is. How this melody comes alive for me now, where before we so often puzzled over its dead letters. Song of a lone person into the far distance, that another of like mind may hear and answer him.

Why can't I send you a sound in the same way, which you would hear at the same hour and answer.

Goodnight my love, I'm tired from all the walking and clambering over bridges. Goodnight.

8 October. After supper.

The good old Doge didn't attend the function at *St Mark's* today, he's ill and instead of the ceremony we visited some other things, we continue to walk about the city seeking out its treasures one after the other.

Palazzo Pisani Moretta. A *Paolo Veronese* that can give you an idea of the master's full worth. It's as fresh as if it was painted yesterday and his great art of producing a delightful harmony without imposing a single tone on the whole piece, merely by the varying areas of colour, is here very evident. As soon as a picture has deteriorated, you can no longer make out any of this.

As far as costume goes, one only has to think he was setting out to paint a sixteenth-century subject and all's well. The younger princess is a charming little mouse and has such a calmly stubborn little face. The rest when we meet.

Scuola di San Rocco. p. 554

These so-called *Scuole* are buildings that belong to the various fraternities, where they hold their meetings and keep the tools of their trade and their treasures. The Fraternity of St Roch got particularly rich after a plague, because pious souls were grateful to this patron saint and the *Santissima Vergine** for saving them from it. It had raged from March to November and now towards winter it stopped all by itself.

Today it really struck me how joyfully human beings embrace something senseless, it only has to be presented to them in sensuous form, so one should be glad to be a poet. What a beautiful invention the Mother of God is, is something you don't feel until you're in the midst of Catholicism. A *Vergine* with the *Son* on her arm, who is however a *santissima Vergine* because she has brought a son into the world. It's a subject that brings your senses to such a beautiful stand-still, it has a kind of inner grace like poetry that gives such pleasure and makes you so unable to think, that it really is made into a religious object.

Unfortunately, though, these subjects have been the scourge of painters and they are the reason why art sank so low again when it had scarcely begun to raise itself. A Danae* is always a quite different task for the artist from an Immaculate Conception and yet ultimately the same subject. Except that the artist can make a great deal out of the first and nothing at all out of the second.

The building of the *Scuola di San Rocco* is grand and beautiful without being an architectural masterpiece. That was still a time for painters. Tintoretto did the big pictures in the main hall. Also a large Crucifixion in a side-room.

My recent observation is being confirmed, but I must explain myself more precisely.

Here too there are large figures excellently painted and the pieces well conceived; but the paintings would all have more charm if they were smaller. The figures, if I can put it like this, appeared to him in a smaller format and he only enlarged them to scale, without being able to enlarge their inner nature.

His human forms, his compositions don't have the *Sodezza** that's required for large figures. They occupy the eye agreeably and render a felicitous idea on a small scale, but they don't have enough inner substance to fill such a large space and to impress with their presence. Thus for example, to make a figure colossal it isn't enough just for it to be nine or ten feet high, its nature must be colossal, it mustn't impress me with its dimensions but with its whole being, so that I don't measure up to it even if I mentally enlarge myself.

The best piece in the hall, I think, is the Lord's Supper by the altar. He's set the table back and in the foreground put in a beggar and a woman sitting on the steps. All the background and the figures in it have an indescribable *Vaghezza*.*

After that I was in the Jewish quarter and in all sorts of other places.

Evening

Today there isn't much to tell you, I was *ai Mendicanti* again where the women perform music, again they sang quite splendidly, especially the one I praised the last time. If only one could keep the impression in one's mind's ear.

Afterwards I was with an old Frenchman who can't speak any Italian and consequently is totally at a loss, despite his letters of recommendation he sometimes doesn't know whether he's coming or going. He's a man of some rank and cultivation to whom I'm very polite and talk about all manner of things, we had a conversation about Venice etc., he asked me how long I'd been here, I told him not yet a fortnight. He replied: *il paroît que Vous n'aves pas perdu votre tems.** That's the first good-conduct certificate I've collected. Tomorrow I'm going to take a long trip away.

If only there were good spirits so that I could make you share just one aria and the moonlight on the water and the square. Goodnight.

9 October

A delightful day from morning to night. I drove to Palestrina, over towards Chiozza* where the large works are that the Republic is putting up against the sea. They're of hewn stone and are really meant to protect the whole strip of land that separates the lagoons from the ocean, a much-needed and very important project. A large map I'm sending will help you grasp what it's all about.

The lagoons are an effect of nature, in the Adriatic gulf there's a considerable stretch of land that is covered and uncovered by the tides. That Venice is what and where it is, with the islands, and the channels that run through the marshes and are navigable even when the tide's out, all this is the doing of human hands; and human hands must preserve it.

The sea can only get into the lagoons at two points, near the castles opposite the Arsenal and at the other end of the *lido* near *Chiozza*. The tide normally comes in twice a day and out again, always by the same route in the same direction, fills the channels and covers the marshy ground, and then flows out again leaving the high ground if not dry then visible, and the channels full.—It would be a quite different matter if it gradually found other routes, attacked the tongue of land, and streamed in and out as and where it pleased. Quite apart from what that would do to the settlements on the *lido*: *Palestrina*, *St Peter*, etc.; the channels in places would overflow, the water would look for new channels, make the *lido* into islands and the islands that presently lie at its centre perhaps into strips of land. To stop this happening, they now have to protect the *lido* all they can. Not just the sea rising, but the way it would arbitrarily attack and overturn what people have taken possession of and what they have given purpose, shape, and direction to.

In extraordinary cases, and there have been some when the sea rose excessively, it's still a good thing if it can get in at two points and the rest are closed off, so it can't get in so fast or with such power and then within a few hours it has to yield to the ebb and in this way too its force is moderated again. Incidentally Venice has no need to worry,* the rate at which the sea-level is slowly dropping gives her thousands of years, and with a little shrewd assistance they will be able to keep the canals filled with water. If only they would keep their city cleaner, which is so necessary and so easy, and really of great importance for ages to come. For example, it's forbidden on pain of severe punishment to tip anything in the canals or throw their sweepings in. But you can't tell a sudden heavy shower not to get into every corner where they've left their sweepings and wash them into the canal. Indeed, what is worse, wash them into the drains that are meant to take the water off so that these get silted up. Even some of the tiles on the Piazzetta by St Mark's, which like the ones on the great Square are a clever device for draining the water away, have sometimes been clogged and flooded. If you get a really rainy day, the result is an intolerable muck. Everyone swears and curses. Going up and down the bridges people splash their cloaks and tabarros, everyone goes about in shoes and stockings and they spray each other, and it's no ordinary muck but really acid. Then the weather turns nice again and nobody thinks about cleanliness. It only needs the *political will*, and something could be done; I'd like to know if they have some political reason for leaving things as they are, or whether it's expensive negligence that lets things slip.

This evening I went up St Mark's tower. Since I'd recently seen the lagoons in all their splendour, with the tide full in, I also wanted to see them in their humbled state when it's out, and it's necessary to combine these two images if you want to have an accurate picture. It looks strange when you see land everywhere where water was before. The islands are no longer islands, but only higher built-up areas in a grey-greenish morass with beautiful channels cutting through it. The marshy part is covered with sea-grass and must also be gradually rising, although the ebb- and flood-tides are constantly tugging and burrowing at it and give the vegetation no peace.

Back to the sea again! Down there today I watched the goings on of the sea-snails, patellas (mussels with a *single* shell) and the pocket-crabs, and it gave me a glow of pleasure observing them. No, really, how delightful and magnificent a *living thing* is! How exactly matched to its condition, how true, how intensely *being*! And how much I'm helped by the small amount of study I've done and how I look forward to taking it further!

Goodnight, my love! I now have a Vitruvius, I must study him so as to achieve illumination. Goodnight.

10 October

Today I've started going through my diary and preparing it for departure. The files are now to be passed to a higher instance for your judgement. I already find that a lot of what I've written could be made more precise, expanded, or improved. Let it stand as a monument to first impressions which, if not always true, we still find delightful and valuable.

I'm also beginning to prepare myself for the close. Iphigenie isn't getting finished; but she shan't lose anything by being with me under these skies. Oh if only I could send you a breath of this light way of being!

For Italians the *Ultramontano** is an obscure idea! as it is for me too. Only you and a few friends wave to me through the mists. Yet I tell you honestly it really is just the climate, otherwise there's nothing that makes me prefer these regions to the north.

For otherwise birth and habit are after all a powerful thing, I wouldn't want to live here, or anywhere else where I didn't have an occupation.

Architecture rises up before me like some ancient spirit from the grave, it tells me to study its principles like the rules of a *dead language*, not so as to practise it or to take a live delight in it, but only so as to revere the eternally departed life of past ages in quiet reflection.

I thank God for the way everything I valued from my young days is becoming dear to me again. How happy I am to be able to get close to Roman history and the ancient writers again! and with what reverent devotion I read Vitruvius!

Now I can say it, can confess my sickness and my foolishness. For years now I haven't been able to look at a Latin author, or touch anything that even just renewed an image of Italy, without suffering the most terrible pain.

Herder used to joke with me that I learned all my Latin reading Spinoza,* for he noticed that was the only Latin text I read. But he didn't know I had to beware of contact with the ancients. Even quite recently Wieland's translation of the *Satires*＊ made me deeply unhappy, I only read two of them and it nearly drove me mad.

If I hadn't taken the resolve that I'm now carrying through, I would have absolutely gone to pieces and become incapable of anything, so ripe had the desire become within me to see these objects with my own eyes. For I could get no nearer through historical knowledge, it was as if the objects were standing there only a hand's-breadth away yet cut off from me by an impenetrable wall.

For it really does feel like that to me now, not as if I were seeing things but as if I were seeing them again. I've been in Venice just this short while, and all Venetian existence is as much part of me as if I'd been here for twenty years. I know too that the idea of it I'm taking away with me, even if it's incomplete, is still certainly a quite clear and true one.

Midnight

Now at last I can really say that I've seen a comedy. Today the *St Luca* Theatre was doing *Le baruffe chiozzotte* which might roughly be translated as *les criailleries de Chiozza* or *Squabblings in Chiozza*.

The characters are all sea-people, inhabitants of Chiozza and their wives and sisters and daughters. There's all the usual to-do of these people, for good or ill, their quarrels, vehemence, manners, easy-goingness, banality, wit, humour etc. are all well caught. The play is a Goldoni* too. As I was in the area only yesterday and the impression of the people's manners and voices was still in my mind's eye and ear, it was great fun, and though there were a lot of jokes I couldn't understand, still I could follow the whole thing very well and had to join heartily in the laughter. But I've also not seen such fun as the people had, seeing themselves and their like put on the stage. Shouts of laughter from beginning to end. But I have to say too that the actors made an excellent job of it. In line with the characters they'd shared out, as it were, the different voices that are found among the people. It took you in from start to finish.

The leading actress was quite exquisite, much better than the other night in heroic garb and high passion. The women in general, but she in particular, imitated the people's voice, gestures, and ways with immense charm.

But it's the author who deserves the highest praise, for giving his countrymen this most enjoyable way of spending an evening, conjured up out of nothing, you can sense everywhere the infinitely practised hand.

11th, evening

I was in the Carità again making a pilgrimage to Palladio's grand inspirations. You could spend years contemplating works like this. Tomorrow morning I'm going back. For I really think I've seen nothing higher. And I feel I'm not mistaken. But just think, the outstanding artist, with an innate feeling for what is great, which he worked hard to cultivate (for people have no idea how much trouble he took over the works of Antiquity) finds an opportunity to carry out a favourite idea, to emulate a dwelling of the ancients, for once the idea exactly fits. There's nothing to get in his way, nor would he let anything. About the invention and the design I say nothing; just this much about the execution. Only the capital and base of the columns and a few other parts, which I took careful note of, are of cut stone. All the rest (I mustn't say of brick) of fired clay, for I've never come across bricks like these, you can imagine how sharp they are, as the frieze with its decoration is also baked from the same material and the various parts of the cornice too. That means he had shapes made for everything in advance, and they must have been much bigger in proportion as the clay shrinks, the parts had all been fired ready and they put the building together just like that with very little lime. The decoration of the arches, everything is fired in the same way. This method wasn't entirely new to me, but the way it's carried through here goes beyond anything I conceived. In Dessau* they did the same, and presumably Palladio had it from the ancients. But precisely for that reason everything is as if all of a piece, if it were whitewashed so that it was all one colour, it would be enchanting. O destiny! to think of the idiocies you favoured and preserved, why didn't you allow this work to be completed?

I don't think I've said anything about a staircase (a spiral staircase without a column in the middle) which he praises himself in his works—*la quale riesce mirabilmente.** You can imagine, if Palladio says *che riesce mirabilmente*, it must be something. Well it's nothing but a spiral staircase, but one that you don't get tired of going up and down. And today I also saw the sacristy, which is right beside the stair and was done to his design, I'm going back again tomorrow. If I could just get it really fixed in my mind and feeling.

The funniest thing is the way I expound all this to my hired servant, because when you're full of a thing, you can't stop talking about it, and you keep looking for some new angle from which to show how wonderful it is.

Farewell. My old Frenchman who's been here a week now is leaving tomorrow, it was a delight to see a dyed-in-the-wool Versailles Frenchman abroad. And he travels, I've been astonished to see in his case just how one can travel, and in his place he's a quite considerable man. Farewell my dearest.

12 October

I stayed at home today to get my things in order, reckon up, read the papers, do some writing, and get myself ready for the next bit of my journey. I've had a thorough look round in the forecourt, let's hope things keep going this well.

My diary will give you the first instantaneous impressions, how nice it will be later on when I can explain in person how all these ideas connect up and lead further, and give you some amusement whenever the time is right.

Yesterday the *St Luca* company were doing a new play, *l'Inglisismo in Italia.** As there are lots of Englishmen living in Italy, it's natural that their manners have some influence, I thought I'd pick up something for future guidance, but it didn't work out. Caricatures as ever, a few good scenes of foolery, but much too heavy and solemnly meant, and aimed only at the lowest level. It didn't even please the audience and was very near to being hissed off the stage.

And then the actors weren't in their element, not in the square at Chiozza.

NB of the Sacchi troupe, which by the by has broken up, I've seen

La Smeraldina. Brighella is still here too, but at *St Grisostomo*, a
theatre that's a bit out of the way for me.

On masks, and the way set characters of that kind take shape by
themselves, more another time.

Farewell for today. My mind's worn out from my lonely day and
so much frantic inactivity.

13 October

Now my dearest I have to close. Tomorrow I'm off, and so is this
packet. I'm weary of seeing and am quietly thinking over what's past
and what's coming next.

However much I've written, there's far more left in my thoughts,
still, most of it has been hinted at.

About the nation itself and the pros and cons of all the nations in
comparison with each other, on the basic character and the dominant
way of life of this one, on the life of the nobility, their houses, their
manners, etc., I'll tell you later, as about much else.

Let it suffice now to send you with great pleasure everything I've
picked up on the way, so that you can judge it for yourself and
preserve it for me for our profit and enjoyment. The first phase of
my journey is past, may heaven bless the ones still to come, and
above all the last one, which will bring me back to you.

The enclosures and drawings I've put in the box that will contain
the coffee. It's the very best quality, from Alexandria, that you can
get here. I'm sending you twenty-five pounds, please give five to the
Duchess with my best compliments and five to the Herders and keep
the rest yourself. If you like it, I can get more.

Farewell. I'm reluctant to close. If everything goes well, you'll get
this before the end of October and the diary of the second phase you
shall have at the end of November. That way I'll be near you again,
and stay near you. Farewell. Greetings to the family. Far and near,
I'm yours.

G.

List of rock-types, contd.

36. Rocks from the Paduan hills which they use for paving in Padua
    and Venice. Is it lava? or porphyry?
37. Limestone that's sawn and variously used for buildings, from
    the foothills of the great chain. *Vitruvius* mentions it.

38. Limestones that have been in the sea for some time and have been eaten away by sea-worms.
39. Sea-mud baked hard. Probably the newest rock-type of all.
40. Basalt debris from the Adriatic.
41. Lime from the wall near *Palestrina*, mixed with tarass.

FIFTH SECTION
FROM VENICE VIA FERRARA/FLORENCE/ PERUGIA, ETC. TO ROME

Venice, 14 October *due ore doppo Notte**

In the last hour of my time here, for I'm leaving tonight with the packet boat to Ferrara. I'm glad to be leaving Venice. To stay here with pleasure and profit I would have to take other steps, which lie outside my plan. Anyway this is the time when everybody leaves town. I shall carry the bizarre, unique image away with me, and much else besides. How good my eye was is for you to decide when I come back and we talk about these things. My journal to date I handed to the coachman today, so it will arrive later than I thought, but I hope at a favourable moment.

I'd like to be able to send you the climate, or transplant you into it. In other ways it wouldn't be much of a life for us here. Farewell. Since Verona I haven't been getting any more distant from you, now I'll be getting further and further away.

Strange! I see from the newspapers that there must have been dreadful weather raging over the mountains. It can't have been more than two days after I crossed them.

Here I've had a few downpours, very heavy one night, with thunder and lightning. This weather comes over from Dalmatia. But it all passes very quickly. The skies are bright again and the clouds fling themselves against the mountains of Friuli, the Tyrol, and Padua. The Florence area had a fearful thunderstorm and a cloudburst. It seems to have been the same one that caught up with me in Verona.

Ferrara, 16th, night

In the lovely great depopulated city where Ariosto lies buried and Tasso suffered misfortune,* I arrived this morning at seven by German time and will leave again tomorrow.

The route I travelled is very pleasant and we had splendid weather. There were some tolerable people on the boat and the outlook and views were charming in a simple way. The Po is a friendly river; it flows through great plains hereabouts and you only see the banks. Here and by the Adige I saw irrigation systems that are quite childish and harmful.

I spent the two nights on deck wrapped in my overcoat; only towards morning did it get cold; I'm now really into the 45th parallel and I repeat, they can keep everything if only like Dido I can take as much of the climate with me as a cowhide will hold* to put round our dwelling. It is a different existence.

I've seen most of what Volkmann talks about on pages 484–489. The picture of Herod and Herodias* is really good. John the Baptist in his usual wilderness costume points at the lady, she looks quite serenely at the king sitting beside her, and the king has his head propped on one hand and is looking with a calm shrewd eye at the Prophet. There's a middling big white dog in front of the King and a little spaniel coming out from under Herodias's skirt, and both the dogs are barking at the Prophet. That strikes me as a nice touch.

Ariosto's grave monument is a lot of marble badly disposed.

Instead of Tasso's prison they show a wooden stall or vault where he certainly wasn't kept. There's hardly anyone in the house who still knows what it is you're looking for.

I'm too tired to tell you any more about a fine academic institute that is protected and funded by a cardinal born in Ferrara.

The Court also has a few delightful old monuments.

Cento, 17th, evening, or as they call it here, night
I'm writing to you from Guercino's* home town, in a better mood than yesterday evening. See especially Volkmann pp. 482–484.

A friendly, well-built little town, population about 5,000, prosperous, bustling, clean, in the middle of an immense plain. I went up the tower, as I always do. A sea of pointed poplars among which in the foreground you can see the small farms, each surrounded by its field. Wonderful soil and a mild climate. It was the kind of evening that makes you thank heaven we have summer evenings.

The sky cleared after being overcast all day, the clouds moved off north and south towards the hills and I hope for a fine day tomorrow.

They have two months of proper winter here, December and January, and a rainy April, otherwise good weather for the season. Never persistent rain. Still, this September was better and warmer than their August.

How delighted I was to see the Apennines today. I'd got thoroughly sick of the plains. Tomorrow I'll write to you from the very foot.

There are some pictures of *Guercino*'s here that you could gaze at for years.

My favourites are:

The risen Christ appearing to his mother. She kneels before him and looks at him with indescribable depth of feeling, she feels his body with her left hand, just beneath the miserable wound that ruins the whole picture. He's put his left hand around her neck and is bending his body back a little to see her close up. That gives the figure something, I won't say constrained, but at any rate alien. Nevertheless it's still infinitely pleasing. And the calm sad expression with which he looks at her, as if his noble mind were filled with the memory of his and her suffering, which isn't healed at once by resurrection.

*Strange** has done an engraving of the picture, so there's some hope you can see a copy of it.

Then comes: a Madonna. The Child wants the breast, and she hesitates bashfully to bare her bosom and give it him. Exquisitely beautiful.

Then Mary with the Child standing up in front of her and looking straight at us, while she guides its arm so that its raised fingers give the blessing. A happy touch, in the sense of Catholic mythology.

Guercino is an inherently sound, manly, robust painter without being crude, rather his pieces have an inner moral grace, a fine freedom and grandeur. And with it a special quality which means that an eye trained on his pictures will not fail to recognize works by him.

So I progress bit by bit. I've pretty well seen the Venetian School, tomorrow I'll be in Bologna, where my eyes shall see Raphael's St Cecilia. But I can't find words to say how strongly Rome draws me. If I gave way to my impatience, I would see nothing on the way and simply hurry straight on. Another fortnight and a yearning of thirty years is stilled. And it still feels as if it were not possible.

Of Guercino's brush I say nothing, it has a lightness and purity and perfection that are unbelievable. He chose particularly beautiful colours shading into brown for the garments.

The other pictures, which I won't list by name, all have more or less unfortunate subjects. The good artist put himself through torments, and still his invention and brushwork, hand and spirit, were squandered and wasted.

I feel glad and rewarded to have seen that as well, although there isn't a lot of enjoyment in rushing past things like this.

Goodnight, my love, I can't concentrate properly again this evening.

You'll forgive the way I just dash things down, at least it's better for later use than an empty page. Goodnight.

18th. Bologna. Evening.
I've taken a decision that makes me feel much more settled. I shall only pass through Florence and make straight for Rome. I don't take any pleasure in anything until that first need is satisfied, in Cento yesterday, here today, it's as if I'm just hastening past for fear that my time is running out, and then, heaven willing, I'd like to be in Rome for All Saints to see the great festival in the right place and I'd better get there a few days in advance, there's nothing for it but to leave Florence out and see it with opened eyes on a happy return.

Bologna too would be worth a long stay.

See Volkmann part 1, pages 375 to 443.

p. 402. *Madonna di Galiera*. Sacristy excellent things.

p. 403. *Giesu e Maria*. Guercino's Circumcision. This disagreeable subject, quite splendidly executed. You can't imagine a better-painted picture. Everything about it is worthy of respect, and it looks as if it were enamel.

425. Palazzo *Tanieri*. The head of Mary as if painted by a god. The expression as she looks down at the Child at her breast indescribable. A calm, profound acceptance as if she were letting the Child—not a child of love and joy, but a changeling foisted on her—just suckle away, because that's the way things are, and in her deep humility she can't understand how she comes to be doing it.

Not much pleasure to be had from the rest of the magnificent figure, the tremendous drapery, marvellously though it's painted, is still just drapery. The colours too have darkened, the room isn't best lit, and it was a dull day.

p. 387. I was at the Institute.* Nothing to say about that. It has a fine noble layout, but in Germany, however *ultramontan* we may be, our collections, academies, teaching methods, etc. are a bit more advanced. Yet to do it justice, it is quite a lot for a single house to have all that to show for itself, available for the common benefit.

This morning on the way over from Cento, between sleeping and waking, I had the good fortune to find the perfect plan for Iphigeneia in Delphi.* There's a fifth act and a recognition scene the like of which there can't be many. I cried like a child over it myself and I hope the treatment will clearly show the Italian influence.

19th. Evening.

I'd like to write you a calm, rational word again now, because the last few days it wouldn't work. I don't know how it will turn out this evening. The world is racing along beneath my feet and a passion beyond words is driving me on. The sight of the Raphael and a walk out towards the hills this evening have calmed me down a bit and gently attached me to this town. I'm telling you everything as I feel it and am not ashamed to confess my weaknesses to you.

First then Raphael's St Cecilia. It is what I knew in advance but now saw with my own eyes. He simply did what others wanted to do. To recognize and appreciate his achievement, and not just to praise him as a god who appeared like Melchizedek without father or mother,* you have to look at his predecessors, his masters. They found a footing on the firm ground of truth, they worked hard, anxiously even, to lay the broad foundations, they competed with one another to build the pyramid higher step by step, until finally he, supported by all these advantages and illuminated by a heavenly genius, put the last stone on the pyramid's highest point which nobody can outtop or even reach again. About the picture when we meet, for the only thing to say is that it's by him. A group of five saints, none of whom are of any concern to us, but whose existence is so perfect that one wishes the picture may last for ever, though content with one's own dissolution.

The older masters I find particularly interesting, also his earliest things. Francesco di *Francia** is a very respectable artist. Peter Perugin* you might almost take for a good honest German.

If only luck had brought Albrecht Dürer across the Alps.* In Munich I saw a couple of pictures by him, of unbelievable greatness. The poor man! instead of his Dutch journey when he picked up that parrot etc. I find it infinitely touching to think of a poor fool of an artist like that, because at root it's my own fate too, except that I'm managing to do something about it.

My pheasant dream* is starting to be fulfilled. For truly, the things I'm loading up with can very well be compared with the most delicious game-birds, and I have a feeling of how it's all going to develop.

In the Ranuzzi Palace I found a St Agatha by Raphael which, though not quite perfectly preserved, is a delightful picture. He has given her a sound, secure, virginal innocence without charm but also without coldness or asperity. I took good note of her and shall read my Iphigenie to this ideal figure and not let my heroine say anything that this saint couldn't say.

About all the rest I'd better say nothing. What is there to say, except that the senseless subjects are enough to drive you mad yourself. It is like when the children of God joined with the daughters of men,* monsters were the result. While you are attracted by the heavenly touch of Guido,* a brush that should only have painted the most perfect things that strike our senses, you want to turn your eyes away from the hideous, stupid subjects which all the abusive words in the world would not be enough to degrade.*

And that's what it's always like.

It's always the dissecting theatre, the gallows' foot, the knacker's yard, always the hero's *sufferings*, never *actions*. Never a present interest, always something fantastical still to come. Either miscreants or ecstatics, criminals or idiots. And that leaves the painter to drag in a naked man or a beautiful female onlooker, in order to salvage something. And he treats his spiritual heroes as mannequins draped in the folds of really beautiful robes. Nothing there that gives an idea of humanity. Of ten subjects, not one that ought to have been painted, and even if there's one, he wasn't allowed to take it from the right angle. The great painting by *Guido* p. 404 is everything that painting can do and everything senseless that can be demanded of a painter, it's a *votive* picture, I believe the whole Senate praised and indeed commissioned it. The two angels, who would be worthy to console a Psyche in her misfortune, here have to—* St Proculus, who was a soldier, is a fine figure, but then the rest of the bishops and parsons.

At the bottom of the picture there are heavenly children playing with allegorical props, etc.

The painter, who had the knife at his throat, did everything he could to show *he* wasn't the barbarian, it was the people who had paid for the picture. Two naked figures by *Guido*, a John the Baptist in the wilderness and a Sebastian, how delightfully painted, and what are they saying? the one has his mouth gaping wide, the other is writhing in agony.

If you take the historical view, you can see that superstition really took control of the arts again and ruined them. But not superstition alone, it was also the narrow requirements of the modern, the northern peoples. For Italy too is still northern and the Romans were really only barbarians who carried off Beauty as you carry off a beautiful woman. They plundered the world and yet needed Greek tailors to fit the tatters to their body. Altogether I can already see the shape of things to come.

Just a word! If someone could only tell the story of some granite column which was first cut in Egypt as part of a temple at Memphis, then dragged off to Alexandria, later made the journey to Rome, was there toppled and erected again after some centuries in honour of a different god. O my love what is the highpoint of all human activity? To me as an artist what is most precious is that it gives the artist a chance to show what is in him and to bring unknown harmonies up from the depths of existence into the light of day.

Two human beings whom I think of as *great* in an absolute sense I have now got to know more closely, Palladio and Raphael. There wasn't a hair's breadth of *arbitrariness* in their work, what makes them so great is that they knew the limits and laws of their art in the highest degree and moved within them and practised them with complete ease.*

Towards evening I was up on the tower. The view is magnificent.

To the north you see the hills by Padua, then the Swiss and Tyrolean and Friulian mountains, in short the whole northern chain, these last in mist this time. Towards evening a limitless horizon with only the towers of Modena standing out, to the east an even plain all the way to the Adriatic which is visible in the mornings, to the south the foothills of the Apennines cultivated to their very tops, with churches, palazzi, garden-houses all over them, as beautiful as the hills by Vicenza. It was a pure cloudless sky, only a kind of height-haze on the horizon. The tower-keeper told me the region hasn't been free of this mist for six years. He used to be able to see the Vicenza hills and the houses on them with his telescope, now that's rare even on the brightest days, and the mist settles all along the northern chain and makes our dear homeland into a true Cimmeria.

He pointed out that you could tell the healthy situation and air of the town from the roofs, which looked like new, the tiles not affected by damp or moss. It's true, they are all clear, but the quality of the tiles may have something to do with it, at least in older times they were made by an expensive firing process.

The hanging tower is a hideous sight, you can't believe your eyes and yet it's very probable that it was deliberately built like that.* It's also made of brick, which is a really excellent method, when you add iron hoops of course you can do all sorts of crazy things.

This evening I took a walk out towards the hills. What beautiful, charming paths and subjects there are. It delighted and somewhat calmed my feelings. I will compose myself too, and wait a bit, if I've been patient these thirty years I shall get through this final fortnight.

The spirits of history are rising hundredfold from their graves and showing me their true shape. I look forward now to reading and thinking through all sorts of things that I used to find unbearable for want of a sensuous conception.

Bologna Italian is a dreadful dialect which I wouldn't have expected here. Rough and abrupt, etc. I don't understand a word when they're talking to each other, Venetian is crystal clear in comparison.

Goodnight. When I go walking I often think of you, and whenever there's anything pleasant, I always imagine it's still possible to make you see it all.

Meanwhile and until I come back, make do with my scribblings.

This evening I've done better than for the last few. Goodnight.

20th, evening.

Today a fine beautiful day which I spent entirely in the open air. As soon as I get back to hills, I have things to tell you about mineralogy.

I rode to Paterno where the Bolognese rock is found, a gypsum spar that glows at night when it's been calcinated.

On the way I found whole cliffs of specular gypsum, No. 2 standing exposed, after I'd passed through an area of sandy-clay rock No. 1.* Near a brick kiln there is a narrow stream with other smaller ones joining it, and at first you think it must be a hill of alluvial clay that the rain has washed down. But I've discovered this much about its character.

The mountain consists of a type of rock No. 3, in itself firm, but composed of fine slaty clay alternating with gypsum. The clayey stone is so completely mixed with pyrites that, where air and moisture get at it, it changes totally, swells up, the layers get lost completely, and it becomes a kind of slate that crumbles like a sea-shell and has a shiny surface like coal No. 4 so that if you couldn't see the stone's two forms in the large pieces (of which I broke up several) you'd hardly believe it. At the same time the shell-like surfaces are covered with white dots, sometimes there are whole yellow sections in them, finally when atmosphere and rain affect the outer part, this gets crumbled into nodules, and the mountain looks like weathered pyrites on a large scale.

Among the layers you also find harder, green and red ones. Nos. 5 and 6. I found kidney-shaped pyrite and precipitates of it on the harder rock No. 7. Whether the gypsum between the rock layers is also phosphorescent would be worth an experiment, I'm bringing some pieces back. 8. NB there's also pure gypsum spar 9. Really though the rock is a calcite that seems to arise in cavities. The clayey rock in its first form contains none, whence I suppose that the phosphorescent gypsum spar only comes about when the rock starts to swell up and leave cavities here and there, the dissolved selenite found in these mountains infiltrates it and permeates it with sulphur. We'll spell all this out better in due course.

A major feature is its weight, which strikes you at once.

I must close for today: I had so much to tell you about what went through my head on this happy day. But it seems heaven has heard my prayers. There's a coach here going to Rome and I shall leave the day after tomorrow. So I must put my things together today and get some work done. Farewell. Today was a perfectly lovely and happy day when the only thing missing was you.

21st, evening
Logano in the Apennine mountains

I was driven out of Bologna* today, and now here I am at a miserable inn in the company of a worthy papal officer on his way home to Perugia and an Englishman with his so-called sister. Goodnight.

22nd, evening. Giredo.

All small Apennine places that I like being in, even if my companions, the English especially, find something to complain about everywhere.

The Apennines are a remarkable part of the world. If these mountains were not too *steep*, if they weren't too *high* above sea level, and not too full of strange twists and turns for the tides in ancient times to have affected them *more* and *longer*, and been able to wash over *larger* areas,* then it would be one of the loveliest of lands. With this most agreeable climate, somewhat higher than the surrounding country, etc.

As it is, though, it's a bizarre weave of mountain ridges at odd angles to each other, where you often can't see which way the water runs off. If the valleys were better filled, the flat country smoother and more washed over, it would be comparable to Bohemia, except that the ridges have in every way a different character.

So you mustn't imagine a mountain wilderness, but largely cultivated mountain country that one travels through. Chestnuts do very well here. They grow excellent wheat, and this year's crop is already standing fine and green. Small-leaved oak trees (holm oaks, I think) line the roads, and there are cypresses round the churches and chapels.

Yesterday evening the weather was dull, today it's fine and bright again.

The *vetturino* is a tolerable means of transport, the best part is that you can comfortably walk along behind it.

My companion is very useful to me, although I'd rather be alone so as to work on Iphigenie. This morning I sat very quiet in the coach and thought out the plan for the great poem on the coming of the *Lord*, or the Wandering Jew.* If heaven would now give me space to gradually carry out all the plans I have in mind. It's incredible the way these last eight weeks have put me on to some major and fundamental ideas about life as well as art.

Did I already tell you that I have a plan for a tragedy Ulysses on Phaea?* A strange idea that could perhaps work.

So Iphigenie has to accompany me all the way to Rome! What will become of the child?

In Bologna I've seen a number of other things about which I'm saying nothing.

A John the Baptist and another Holy Family by Raphael and a few works by Guido and the Carraccis* which are excellent.

I met an Englishwoman enveloped in a kind of prophet's cloak copying a Guido. How I wish you could have the pleasure of doing the same.

There are some heads by the Spaniard Velasquetz* here. He made real advances. I saw a nice touch in a statue of Andromeda. She stands with her hands bound above her almost on tiptoe and to give the figure some support the artist has a small Cupid kneeling beside her holding her foot with his left hand and aiming an arrow at the monster (which naturally is only imagined as present). I liked this idea, it's simple and graceful and basically just a mechanical aid to help the statue stand.

Goodnight. It's cold and I'm tired. Goodnight! When shall I actually say those words to you again!

25th, evening. Perugia.

I haven't written for two evenings, it wasn't possible, our hostelries were so awful that there was no chance of spreading out a page to write on. I've a lot to catch up. Although the second phase of my journey from Venice to Rome will certainly be less full of things to narrate, for more than one reason.

23rd. At ten in the morning our time, we emerged from the Apennines and saw Florence lying in a broad plain, which is unbelievably densely cultivated and strewn with houses and villas.

About the city I'll say nothing, it's been described countless times. I just went through the Bovoli pleasure garden, which is beautifully situated, also the cathedral and the baptistry, two buildings that have not yet exhausted the wit of man.

You only have to look at the city to see the wealth that built it, and the effect a succession of fortunate rulers has had.

In general it's striking what a handsome, imposing look public works like roads and bridges have in Tuscany, it's all like a doll's house.

What I was saying earlier about how the Apennines could be, Tuscany actually is. Because it was so much lower-lying, the ancient seas did their job and heaped up a depth of alkaline soil, it's pale yellow and very easy to work, they plough deep but still absolutely in the old original way. Their ploughs don't have wheels, so the peasant drags along following his oxen and churns the earth up. They do up to five ploughings. Little and light manure, as far as I've seen, and that they scatter by hand. True children of nature, as we shall see further from the description of their character. Finally they sow the wheat and then they heap up long narrow beds with deep furrows between, all so arranged for the rainwater to run off. The crop then grows up out of the top of the heaps. They go along the furrows to do the weeding. I still can't quite understand why they leave so much space free. In some places I suppose where they have reason to fear it will get too wet, but they do it on the finest broad open areas too. I haven't yet been given a thorough account.

Near Arezzo a magnificent plain opens up, where I observed apropos the said fields and the methods of cultivation:

You couldn't get a finer tilth, no clumps of earth, everything clear. But you also don't see ploughed-in straw, wheat however does well. And it suits its nature here. The second year they plant beans for the horses, which aren't fed oats. Lupins are also sown, which are now well up and green and will fruit in March. Flax is already sown and sprouting too, it grows through the winter and the frost only makes it hardier, it wouldn't stand our winters. The olive trees are wonderful plants. When they're old they look almost like willows, like them they lose their heartwood and the bark breaks up. But they have a firmer, more vigorous appearance. You can see by looking at the wood that it grows very slowly, and that it has an intricate inner structure. The leaf is also willow-like, only with fewer leaves to the twig. On the hills around Florence there are olives and vines growing everywhere and in the space between they grow cereal crops. Near Arezzo and over that way they leave the fields clearer. I don't think they do enough to discourage the ivy, which lives off the olive as much as other trees. It would be a simple matter. You see no meadows at all. They say that since maize was introduced it has greatly impoverished the soil. I can believe it, seeing how little manure they put in. I pick up all this just driving by, and do feel very pleased to be seeing the beautiful country even though the discomforts are great. I continue to look carefully at the land itself, also at its inhabitants, their culture, their relations among themselves, and finally at myself as a foreigner and what it comes to mean to him and how.

Here it occurs to me that I must praise the Tuscan *customs arrangements* which are good and efficient, even though they caused me some trouble, and the others that gave me no trouble are useless.

My travelling companion is a Count Cesare from hereabouts, a very good kind of person, and a real Italian too.

As I was often silent and lost in thought, he once said: *che pensa? non deve mai pensar l'uomo pensando s'invecchia*; and after some conversation: *non deve fermarsi l'huomo in una sola cosa, perche allora divien matto, bisogna aver mille cose, una confusione nella testa.**

What do you think of my philosopher and can you imagine how it made me smile, old *Mambrès, toujours faisant de profondes réflexions.**

This evening we bade each other farewell, with the assurance that I would visit him in Bologna, where he is stationed, on my way back.

I'm just writing what comes into my head, it's cold and out in the main room some merchants from Fuligno are eating by the fire, I go across from time to time to get warm.

Here again there's lots to see that I'm deliberately leaving on one side, before I get to Rome I don't want to open my eyes or get excited. Still three days to go, and I feel as if I'll never arrive.

(Here a few remarks that belong higher up.

Wine needs thin nourishment on hillsides and a lot of sun, in the plain it gets too heavy. The moisture that encroaches can't be boiled off sufficiently, that produces a crude beverage.

Near Ferrara I noticed that they scatter the highway with broken bricks, that's excellent and the old bricks that have no other purpose get used. They're also very good for garden paths, as soon as I get back I intend to experiment with both.)

Tuscany seems to me well run, everything looks as if it's been *completed*. Everything is ready for practical benefit and for higher purposes.

On the way back we'll have a closer look.

The Papal State seems to keep going because it can't go under.

The lake at Perugia is a beautiful sight. I long to have one of my close friends at my side. How unlucky the Duke is that other passions prevent him from undertaking a journey that he could make in comfort and with pleasure.*

If I were to do this journey again, I'd also know better now. What with the different kinds of money, the prices, the coachmen, the bad inns, it's a constant bother every day, so that someone who's here for the first time and travelling alone like me, seeking and hoping for uninterrupted enjoyment, would be bound to be unhappy enough. I didn't want anything except to see the country at whatever cost, even if they take me to Rome on Ixion's wheel;* I really don't much mind. When I've talked to Tischbein,* then I'll describe the Italians in the mass as I've seen them. Then you can set that alongside other accounts.

This writing is dreadful, please put it down to the cold and the awkwardness of the table I'm writing at. I've thought so much *for you* these last two days that I'd like to get at least something down on paper.

If one wants to see in reality the first poetic idea that mankind mostly lived in the open air and only sometimes withdrew into caves under pressure of need, then the buildings round here, especially in the country, are the ones to look at. Exactly the feel and flavour of caves.

They have an incredible nonchalance *per non invecchiarsi.** For example, some time I must do you a description of a *vetturino* coach and its genealogy as I've worked it out, and it doesn't occur to anyone to make this mode of transport more convenient, more comfortable for human beings and animals, more advantageous for its owner, and all it would need is a trifle which any other country would have found fifty years ago.

Now goodnight. Can't manage more. I am deeply devoted to you and really longing for you; I'm already beginning to be worried by the snow that will soon powerfully come between us. Goodnight.

26th, evening.

This evening I had an overwhelming desire to write to you and can't satisfy it.

I'm in

Fuligno

in a positively Homeric household, where everyone is gathered round a fire in a great hall, shouting and making a racket and eating at long tables, just like paintings of the wedding feast at Cana. Somebody has just sent for an inkpot and I'm seizing the chance to say a quick word to you.

I saw nothing in Perugia, by chance and by my own fault. The situation of the town is beautiful and well fixed in my mind.

The way here first went downhill, then off down a lovely valley shut in on both sides in the far distance. Finally there was Assissi before us. My Volkmann talked about the Maria della *Minerva*,* I got out at Madonna del Angelo and left my coachman to make his way on to Fuligno, I climbed up to Assisi against a strong wind. I didn't take in *il Gran Convento* and the honoured sacred gallows hill,* didn't see the burial-place of St Francis, like Cardinal *Bembo*￼* I didn't want to ruin my imagination, but asked a nice-looking lad where the Maria della Minerva was. He took me there and we had to climb all the way up through the town, which is built on a hill. Finally we came to the old town proper, and behold! there stood the lovely sacred work. Such a modest temple as befitted such a small town, and yet so *complete* and conceived in a style that would look well anywhere.

And not the temple only, Volkmann can describe that for you, but its position.

Since reading Vitruvius and Palladio on how towns ought to be built and temples placed etc., I have a great respect for these things.

So natural, and so great in their naturalness.

First it stands on the finest elevation, in the place that is still the *town square*, it's just where two hills join, the square itself rises a bit and four streets come together which make a very compressed St Andrew's cross. Two streets coming up from below, two down from above. Probably in olden times there were no houses opposite the temple, it faces due south and if you imagine it without the houses, it had the most beautiful view. The streets must be original ancient, more or less, for they follow from the lie of the hill. Now I couldn't rightly understand why the temple didn't stand in the middle of one side of the square, in the end I worked it out.

The road that comes up from Rome was already built, I assume, and the architect angled the temple so that what you sighted as you came up the road was not the whole temple but one side of it.

I'll do you a small sketch, if I can manage it, to make this clear. It was the greatest pleasure to find that the temple (I mean of course the façade) confirmed my ideas and corroborated my principles.

It is of the Corinthian order, with the columns spaced, I would judge, a bit more than two diameters apart. The columns stand on their own bases, and in addition on cubes, then pedestals, but the pedestals are really the divided base of the whole building, for there are five sets of steps going up between the columns.* *Five*, because

the ancients usually had uneven numbers of steps. Beneath all this there were more steps going down, which I couldn't observe because they were partly buried, partly covered with paving-stones. This way of dividing the building's base and bringing the steps up is something I've never approved of, but here it was right, for the confined space of the square forced the architect to set his steps in. So even the best engraving can't tell us as much as seeing things on the spot.

(They're making such a row all round me that I can scarcely go on writing.)

It's just this that was the way of ancient artists, which I have more of a feel for than ever, that like nature itself they could adapt to any situation and still manage to produce something true, something live.

Afterwards I had a marvellous evening, I went from Assissi to Foligno on foot and communed only with *you*, now the Italians are filling my ears with so much noise that I can't say a word.

When I saw the poor peasants laboriously turning over the stones here too, I thought of your Kochberg estate* and said to myself with heartfelt tears: when shall I enjoy a lovely evening in Kochberg with her again? I tell you my love, if they didn't have the advantage here of a better climate!

Their incredible carelessness in not making proper preparations for the winter means they suffer bitterly. We'd make a better job of it.

Goodnight my love. The noise is dying down, I've stuck it out. But I'm weary.

My evening walk was quite lovely. A full four hours along a hill-side with a beautiful cultivated valley on my right.

I get along very well with the people, and given a year's practice and a moderate amount of money I reckon I'd be on top of things. But it isn't worth the trouble of changing one's whole existence.

When I think to myself today's Thursday and next Sunday you'll be sleeping in Rome after thirty years of wishing and hoping. What a foolish thing is man. I'm sorry, there's a terrible draught coming through the windows, I'm just rambling on. Goodnight.

                                            27th, evening. Terni.
Sitting in another cave that suffered an earthquake a year ago, I address my prayer to you, my dear guardian spirit.

Only now do I feel how spoilt I am. Ten years living with you, being loved by you, and now in an alien world. I told myself how it would be, and only extreme necessity compelled me to take the decision. Let us have no other thought but to pass the rest of our lives with each other.

Terni lies in a delightful region, which I had the pleasure of surveying this evening on a walk round the outside of the town. Since Perugia when Count Cesare and I parted, I've had a priest for company. By coming into contact with new people all the time, I'm very much achieving my aim and I assure you, hearing them talk among themselves really gives you a living image of the whole country. Among themselves they have such a strong national and *town* feeling, they can't any of them stand each other, the social classes are all the time at loggerheads, and all with a constant live and present passion, so that they lay on all-day comedy and have no secrets from the onlooker. I've climbed up to Spoleto and been on the aqueduct, which is also a bridge from one hill across to the other. The ten arches that fill the valley have been quietly standing there with their bricks for centuries and the water in Spoleto still gushes out at every turn. That's the third work of the ancients I've seen now, and once again so beautifully natural, apt for its purpose and true. That marvellous flair they had! Let it be, we'll talk more about it. I've always so hated arbitrary 'designs'. That winter barn of a place at Weissenstein,* much ado about nothing, an enormous stuck-on confection, and it's the same with thousands of other things. Whatever has no true inner existence has no life, and cannot be brought alive, and cannot be great or become great.

The next four weeks* will be full of joys and travail for me, I shall get hold of what I can. This much I can say for sure, that I haven't yet got hold of any wrong ideas. It seems arrogant, but I know it's so, and I know what it costs me to take and grasp only what is true.

St Crucifisso in my opinion isn't really the remains of a temple (that is, of a temple that stood *like that*), rather they found columns, pillars, entablatures, and stuck them together, not stupid so much as crazy. A description would take too long and it isn't worth it.

Roman history is starting to feel as if I was there when it happened.* How I shall study it when I get back, now I know the cities and mountains and valleys! But what I now find infinitely fascinating is the Etruscans. I couldn't see the Raphael in Foligno, it was already dark, here I couldn't see the waterfalls, it was nearly so. At a first cursory reading of Italy I needn't and can't take everything with me. Rome! Rome!—I no longer get undressed, so as to be ready to leave straight away in the morning. Just two more nights! and if the angel of the Lord doesn't strike us down on the way, we shall be there.

As I climbed out of Bologna into the Apennines, the clouds were still moving north. For the first time I saw them moving south towards the lake of Perugia and *here* they also stick and then move south. All that fits my hypothesis very nicely. And where in summer the great plain of the Po sends all its clouds towards the Tyrolean mountains, it now sends a part of them towards the Apennines, more still in the winter (the other clouds also stay static) hence the rainy season.

The rock as far as here stays the same with few variations. Always the old limestone, the seams and beds have got more and more visible over these last few stages.

Trevi lies at the edge of a lovely plain between mountains, it's all still limestone. I couldn't detect anything volcanic. But like Bologna on the far side, it's right at one extreme on this side. Perhaps something will crop up tomorrow. Volkmann says so.

They're starting to harvest the olives now, here they pick them by hand, in other places they knock them down.

If winter comes while they're still at it, the remaining olives stay on the trees almost till spring. Today I saw the biggest and oldest olive trees on very stony ground.

This morning there was a really keen wind blowing, by evening it was beautiful again, and it will be fine tomorrow. Goodnight my dearest. I hope you have my Venice letter by now.

Città Castellana. 28 October.

I mustn't miss out this last evening, it's not yet eight o'clock and everyone's in bed. I almost followed their bad example.

Today was a perfectly fine splendid day, the morning very cold, the day clear and warm, the evening a bit windy but beautiful.

We left Terni very early. As I sleep in my clothes, there's nothing I like better than to be woken before dawn, get into the coach, and drive off between sleeping and waking to meet the day. Today my muse blessed me again with a good idea.

We went up towards Narni before daybreak, I didn't see the bridge. From there on, valleys and depths, near views and distant prospects, delightful regions, all limestone, never a trace of any other rock.

Otricoli lies on a gravel hill long ago built up by the Tiber and is made of lavas that have been brought over from beyond the river.

After crossing the bridge, page 365, you can tell at once you're on volcanic terrain. You go up a hill that consists of grey lava with white so-called garnets.* The highway that runs from the summit down to Città Castellana is made of this same lava, worn beautifully smooth by wheels, the ground is now wholly volcanic.

The town stands on volcanic tufa which consists as usual of ash, pumice, and lava fragments, nearer to the town I didn't see that lava again.

From the castle there's a fine view. The hill S. Oreste (Soracte) is (in my opinion) a limestone outrider of the Apennines on and around which volcanic fires have raged. The volcanic stretches are much lower than the Apennines and only water breaking through made them into hills and cliffs, there are some fine subjects there, though, overhanging rocks etc.

Goodnight now. Tomorrow evening in Rome. After that I have nothing more left to wish for but to see you and my few friends again in good health.

Rome 29 October. Evening.

My second word shall be to you, after heartfelt thanks to heaven for bringing me here.

I can say nothing now except I am here, I've sent word to Tischbein.

Night

Tischbein has been. A thoroughly nice man. Only now do I begin to live, and give reverent thanks to my guiding Genius.

More tomorrow.

30th. Night

Just a word after a very full day! I saw the most important ruins of ancient Rome this morning, this evening St Peter's and am now initiated.

I've moved in with Tischbein and now have relief from all the life of inns and travel. Farewell.

50. Various kinds of limestone chipped off in the Apennines.
51. Kind of travertin found near Terni of wholly volcanic soil, probably from a building.
52. Limestone with iron from the Apennines.
53. Apennine granite. Cut from a loose piece.
54. Lava with white garnets. Just this side of the bridge over the Tiber from Otricoli to Città Castellana.

GOETHE'S LETTERS FROM ITALY

A Selection of Extracts

1. *To his Weimar friends, 1 November 1786*

At last I've arrived in this capital of the ancient world! . . . Now I'm here and at peace with myself and, it seems, at peace for the whole of my life. For it can well be called the start of a new life when you see with your own eyes the whole thing of which you knew so thoroughly the separate parts. I now see all the dreams of my youth come alive, I am now seeing for real the first engravings I can remember (my father had views of Rome hanging in an ante-chamber) and everything I have for so long known in paintings and drawings, engravings and woodcuts, plaster and cork, now stands before me in one piece, wherever I go I find an acquaintance in a new world, it is all just as I imagined it and all new. I can say the same about my observations and ideas. I have had no entirely new thoughts, found nothing wholly strange to me, but the old thoughts have become so definite, so alive, so coherent, that they can count as new.

When Pygmalion's Elise,* whom he had shaped to his wishes and given as much truth and existence as an artist can, at last came towards him and said: Now I really *am*! how different was the living woman from the fashioned stone.

2. *To the Duke Carl August, 3 November 1786*

Forgive my secretiveness and the virtually subterranean journey here. I hardly dared to tell myself where I was going, even on the way I was still afraid, and only at the Porta del Popolo did I feel sure of having Rome. And let me now say too that I think of you a thousand times, no, constantly, when I am near the objects that I never thought I would see without you. Only when I saw that you were chained body and soul in the north, and all fancy for these regions had vanished, was I able to resolve on a long, lonely journey and go in search of the objects which I was drawn to by an irresistible need. In fact these last years it became a kind of sickness which only the sight

---

Unless otherwise indicated, all letters are from Rome. For addressees, see 'Goethe's Circle and Correspondents'.

of things in their real presence could heal. Now I can confess it, at the end I no longer dared look at a Latin book or a drawing of some part of Italy. The desire to see this country was overripe, only now that it's satisfied do I once more feel a deep affection for friends and homeland and the wish to return.

3. *To his mother,* * 4 November 1786*

Today I don't have time to say much, I just wanted you to share my pleasure at once. I shall come back as a new man and live to my own and my friends' greater pleasure.

4. *Her reply, 17 November 1786*

Dear Son, An apparition from the underworld couldn't have astonished me more than your letter from Rome—I could have shouted with joy when I heard that the wish you've cherished from childhood has now come true. A person such as you are, with all that you now know, your grand, pure perception of everything that is good, great, and beautiful, you with your eagle's eye—a journey like this must make you contented and happy for the whole of the rest of your life—and not you alone but all who have the good fortune to live in your sphere of activity.

5. *To Charlotte von Stein, 7–11 November 1786*

From Venice to Rome I wrote another section of diary, that will arrive with Iphigenie, I wanted to go on writing a diary here, but it didn't work. Travelling you pick up what you can, every day brings something and you hastily think it through and arrive at a judgement. Here you're in an immense school where a single day says so much, and yet you don't dare say anything about the day. . . . If you, with your eye and your pleasure in the arts, were to see the things there are here, you would get immense pleasure from it, because for all the heightening and embellishing effects of imagination, one still doesn't have any idea of the True. . . . But the greatest thing, and what I only feel now I'm on the spot: anyone who seriously looks about him here and has eyes to see must become *solid*, he must get an idea of solidity such as never before struck him so forcefully. For me at least it is as if I had never had such a right perception of the things of this world as I do here.

6. *To Johann Gottfried and Caroline Herder, 10–11 November 1786*

At last I have reached the goal of my wishes and am living here with a clarity and calm that you can imagine because you know me. My practice of seeing and reading things as they are, of faithfully letting 'mine eye be single',* my complete renunciation of all fixed views, are here giving me a quiet happiness of the fullest kind. Every day a new remarkable object, daily new, grand, strange images and a coherent whole that one had long thought and dreamed of but the extent of which no imagining could encompass. . . . What gives me the deepest delight is the way I can feel it affect my whole being: there is an inner solidity which is so to speak imprinted on the mind; a mood that is serious without being dry, and settled yet touched with joy.* I think the result will be blessings on my whole future life.

When you look at a phenomenon that is 2,000 years old and more, changed so profoundly and in so many ways by the vicissitudes of time, and yet still the same ground, the same hill, indeed often the same column and wall, and among the people still traces of the old character: then you feel you are sharing in the great decisions of destiny.

7. *To Carl Ludwig von Knebel, 17 November 1786*

There are as you know few traces left of the private life of the ancients, all the greater are the remains that show their concern for the people and the common weal and their true greatness as lords of the then world. I've already seen and re-seen the most remarkable of these things. Aqueducts, baths, theatres, amphitheatres, racecourses, temples! And then the imperial palaces, the graves of the great—these are the images with which I have been nourishing and strengthening my mind. I read Vitruvius so as to feel on my face the breath of the time when all this was just rising out of the earth.

8. *To his Weimar friends, 22 November 1786*

Then we went to the Sistine Chapel . . . Our admiration was divided between the Last Judgement and the many other ceiling paintings by Michelangelo. I could only look in amazement. The master's manly style and intuitive grand sureness of touch, his greatness are beyond words.

9. *To Charlotte von Stein, 24 November 1786*

It is a good and necessary thing when you come here to maintain a
Pythagorean silence.* I could spend years here without saying much.
It's all been so thoroughly and learnedly described already that the
thing you need to do first is open your eyes and learn. You know my
old way of treating nature, that's how I'm treating Rome, and already
it's rising to meet me, I keep on with seeing and thorough study. . . .
I've wanted an element like this for a long time, so I too could swim
for once and not always wade.

10. *To his Weimar friends, 2 December 1786*

Altogether there's nothing to compare with the new life that a
thoughtful person gets from the experience of a new country.
Though I'm still the same man, I think I'm changed to the inmost
marrow of my bones.

I'll close for now and my next letter shall be filled for once entirely
with disaster, murder, earthquake, and misfortune, to add some
shadows to my picture.

11. *To the Herders, 2–9 December 1786*

But still these magnificent objects are like new acquaintances to me,
one hasn't lived with them, not compared them enough. Some of
them seize hold of you so violently that for a time it makes you
indifferent, unjust towards others. Thus the Pantheon façade, the
Apollo of Belvedere, a number of immense heads, and most recently
the Sistine Chapel have so occupied my mind that I scarcely see
anything else beside them. You know me and can easily imagine that
I'd need a year to get so few but great objects straight in my mind.
But then there's an immense number of outstanding works that
press in on you from all sides, you encounter them at every turn, and
they all demand the tribute of your attention. I'll have to see how I
can cope.

By chance I found Archenholz's *Italy* here. I can't tell you how
that kind of screed positively shrinks when seen on the spot. It's as if
you were to put the volume on hot coals so it gradually turns brown
and black, the pages curl and go up in smoke. He saw the things, but
along with his bragging and dismissive manner he possesses too little
knowledge and bumbles about, indiscriminately praising and
damning.

All the time I'm here I shall open my eyes, modestly look and wait and see what takes shape in my mind.

Winckelmann's *History of Art*,* the new Italian edition, is very usable, I'll bring it back with me. . . .

It's a marvel how much is being packed into this year. It's a healthy sign and a real blessing that life is stirring in me again after a long blockage. I feel very, very different and better.

Now I'm starting to take pleasure in Roman antiquities, history, inscriptions, coins, etc., which I previously couldn't be bothered with, everything is coming to life and pressing in on me. The way things were with my study of natural history is how it is again here.

This place has links with the whole history of the world, and I count a second birth, a true rebirth from the day I set foot in Rome.

In the five weeks since I arrived, I've seen a lot of foreigners come and go. Thank God that in future none of these birds of passage will impress me when they talk about Rome, they won't stir me up inside any more; for I've now seen it too, and know where I am. My resolute incognito saves me a lot of time, I visit absolutely no one except artists. The only exception is Count Harrach's brother, who has been very obliging in getting me in to see things that can't normally be seen. With his help I hope to get into a nunnery where there are remains of a temple to Mars, that should be very interesting.

12. *To Carl August, 12–16 December 1786*

I keep on walking about Rome till I'm almost exhausted, and I have *seen* most things. But what is *seeing*, with things you need to linger over and keep going back to so as to get to know them and appreciate them . . . By Christmas my programme in Rome will be completed for the time being, in the New Year I'm going to Naples to enjoy the splendours of nature and cleanse my mind of the idea of so many sad ruins, and have some relief from the all-too-severe principles of art. . . .

So much presses in on me from every side and every angle that I hardly know where I am. But it's a pleasure to live in such a grand element where you see nourishment for many years in front of you, even if for the moment you can only taste it with the tips of your lips.*

13. *To the Herders, 13 December 1786*

I'm gradually recovering from my *salto mortale** and studying more than I'm enjoying myself. Rome is a world, and you need years even just to get your bearings in it. Happy the travellers who just see and go. This morning I picked up the letters Winckelmann wrote from Italy. With what emotion I started to read them! He came here thirty-one years ago, in the same season, an even poorer fool than me, and he was so earnestly German about making a thorough and solid study of art and Antiquity. What sterling good work he did from first to last! And what the memory of this man means to me in this place.

14. *To Charlotte von Stein, 13–16 December 1786*

Since arriving in Rome I have tirelessly seen everything worth seeing and filled my mind with it to overflowing, just when a lot of things seemed to be settling and becoming clear, your note arrived and broke it all off for me. I saw a few more villas, some ruins, with my eyes merely. When I realized I was no longer seeing anything, I stopped and just mooned about.

15. *To Duchess Louise, 12–23 December 1786*

I have now finished the first fleeting rush through Rome, I know the city and its situation, the ruins, villas, palaces, galleries, and museums. With such a profusion of objects it is so easy to think, feel, or fantasize something. But when it comes to seeing things for their own sake, penetrating the arts to the core, judging everything shaped and created not on the effect it produces in us but by its inherent worth, then indeed one feels how hard the task is and wishes one could devote more time and more serious contemplation to these valuable monuments to the human spirit and human endeavour.

In order to neglect nothing I immediately sacrificed a part of the initial pleasure and saw the ruins in the company of architects, other works of art with other artists, and was able to see that a lifetime of activity and practice is scarcely enough to bring our knowledge to the highest point of purity. And yet only the confident certainty that we are taking things for what they are, able to place even the best of them in proper order and consider each in relation to the others, would be the greatest enjoyment to which we should aspire in art as in nature and life.

16. *To Charlotte von Stein, 20–3 December 1786*

I'm now beginning to see the best things for the second time, when you get past the first astonishment and start to just live with things, with a more intimate sense of their value. I let everything come to meet me and don't force myself to find this or that in the object. I am now looking at art in the way I've previously looked at nature, am gaining—what I've long striven for—a fuller idea of the highest creations of humankind, my mind is developing in this direction too and has clear water before it.

There are some objects it isn't possible to have any conception of without having seen them, seen them in marble, the Apollo of Belvedere surpasses anything you can imagine, and the supreme breath of the living being in its youthful freedom and eternal freshness vanishes at once in even the best plaster cast. . . .

And yet it all gives me more labour and worry than enjoyment. The rebirth that is transforming me from within goes on having its effect, of course I thought I would learn something here, but I had no idea I would have to go back to school at so basic a level and *un*learn so much. . . .

That you were ill, ill through my fault, pains me more deeply than I can say. Forgive me, it was a life-and-death struggle and no tongue can express what was going on inside me, this tumble has brought me to myself. My love! My love! . . . My diaries must arrive in the end* and bring you my heart, tell you that you are my only one and share me with nobody.

17. *To Charlotte von Stein, 29–30 December 1786*

I'm like an architect who wanted to put up a tower and had laid a poor foundation; he realizes it in time and is glad to take down what he's built, so as to make the ground more secure, and rejoices in advance at the greater strength of his building. That I've studied nature so keenly and thoroughly in the last few years now helps me with art too. Heaven grant when I come back that you will feel the moral advantages life in a wider world has brought me.

Since I can't take a complete idea of Italy away with me, I at least want to see what I see with my own eyes and in my own way. It will be the same for me with this country as it is with my favourite sciences. Everything depends on seeing things right first time off, the rest follows, and written tradition doesn't give that flair for seeing things right. But now I'll gladly read and listen and collect relevant materials, for I can have my own thoughts as I do, I have a basis for judgement.

18. *To Herder, 29–30 December 1786*

I've taken a break for a while in *seeing*, so as to let what I'd seen take effect. Now I'm starting again and it's going brilliantly. But I also have to admit that I'm giving up all old ideas and all my individual will so as to be properly reborn and reschooled.

The ability to discover similar conditions, however remote they may be from one another, and to trace the genesis of things,* helps me enormously here too.

19. *To Fritz von Stein, 4 January 1787*

I'm writing to you muffled up in my big cloak and with my fire-pot by me, for my room has neither fireplace nor stove and since yesterday there's been a north wind. The weather is fine and it's nice to go out walking in the dry streets.

Now I must tell you all sorts of stories. Recently in St Peter's we almost, as they say, fell over the Pope. We were strolling round the church after lunch and looking at the different kinds of stone with which the interior is decorated. Tischbein was just showing me an exceptionally beautifully designed alabaster (more precisely calcspar) on a gravestone, when I said in his ear: *there's the Pope*. It really was His Holiness, kneeling by a pillar in a long white robe with the red cord and praying. The Monsignores of his retinue, one of them holding the red gold-braided hat, were standing not far off with their breviaries and talking together, and instead of a solemn silence the people who do the cleaning in St Peter's were making a continual noise so that the Pope would notice them and see how busy they were, for once he'd gone they went back to doing nothing.

When you meet the Pope, wherever it happens to be, you kneel down to receive the blessing. He doesn't have a beard, but looks as he does on that cameo reproduction, only older. Nobody wears a beard here except the Greek priests and the Capuchins.

Now another scene. We recently saw, and I can tell you heard, a thousand pigs being slaughtered in a large pen. This happens all winter through, every Friday, in a square where a temple to Minerva once stood. The pigs are boxed in by the hundred between bars; at a given signal men jump in among the animals, seize them, wrestle with them, and stab them under one of the front trotters with a round iron implement which, having a kind of protruding piece on the top, can be twisted in the wound with the flat of the hand till the animal is dead. The racket the men made, which was almost drowned by the cries of the animals, the squabbles that arise in the process, the involvement of the onlookers, and all sorts of other details make this *amazzamento** the strangest of spectacles. It's done like this because everything here is a monopoly and the government buys up the pigs, has them slaughtered, and then distributes them to butchers.

Then I was at the first night of an opera where the groundlings made even more noise than the pigs, I'll tell you the details one day. . . . I also have to tell you that I was pronounced a *Pastore dell' Arcadia** when I went to this society today. I tried in vain to decline this honour because I don't want to reveal my identity. I had to have very handsome comments read out to me and I received the name Megalio *per causa della grandezza* or *grandiosità delle mie opere*,* as the gentlemen of the society chose to express it. If I get the sonnet that was also read out in my honour, I'll send it you.

20. *To Charlotte von Stein, 6 January 1787*

I'm already much improved psychologically, I've already given up many ideas I was attached to that made me and others unhappy, and I feel much freer. I daily slough off another layer and hope to return as a human being. But do now help me too, and meet me halfway with your love. . . . There's nothing I need to look for in the world but what is already found, only I must learn to enjoy it, that's all I'm having myself hammered and reworked for. . . .

Since yesterday I have a colossal head of Juno in my room, or rather the front part, the face. This was my first love in Rome and now I possess the object of my wishes. I'd love to be looking at it with you beside me. I'll certainly bring it back to Germany and how we will enjoy a presence like that! Words can't convey any idea of it; it's like Homer's poetry. . . . Today being Epiphany, I saw and heard Mass conducted according to the Greek rite. Tell Herder. The ceremonies are, or rather seem to me, more theatrical, more pedantic, more reflective, and yet more popular than the Latin. As a particular favour I had a place in the sanctuary and saw the play from within.

There too I realized that I am too old for anything that is not simply true. Their ceremonies and operas, processions and ballets, all run off me like water off a duck's back. An effect of nature, a work of art like the much-revered Juno, are the only things that can make a deep and lasting impression.

21. *To his Weimar friends, 6 January 1787*

I am cured of an enormous passion and sickness, restored to the healthy enjoyment of history, poetry, the monuments of Antiquity, and have a store that I can spend years developing and completing. . . . But now there's Sicily down there. The journey would need a bit of preparing before I undertook it in the autumn, and it would have to be not a mere trip once round and through, which is quickly done but only gives you for all your trouble and money the right to say 'I've seen it.' One would really need to settle in properly in Palermo and then in Catania to make specific and useful excursions . . .

But all these prospects are overshadowed by the Duke's accident.* Since I had the letters about it I've had no rest, and would soonest leave immediately after Easter, loaded with the fragments of my conquests, have a quick look at northern Italy, and be back in Weimar in June. I don't feel able to take that decision by myself, and am describing my whole situation fully so that you can kindly decide on my fate in a council of those who love me and know me best, with the premiss that, as I can truly say, I am more inclined to return than to stay on. What keeps me in Italy most is Tischbein. Even if I'm destined to visit this beautiful land a second time, I shall never be able to learn so much in so short a time as I am now doing in the company of this trained, experienced, perceptive, authoritative man who is attached to me body and soul. I won't say how the scales fall from my eyes. When you're wandering about at night, you think dawn is daylight and a grey day is bright, but then what about when the sun rises?

22. *To Philipp Friedrich Seidel, 13 January 1787*

Give the enclosed package to Herr Herder, it contains Iphigenie . . . I am well, the very fine weather means you can make use of the whole day, I've practically seen my way through all of Rome and am now repeating, already things seen are beginning to fall into place and what seemed endless is settling within bounds. Even so the field is too great and you can't get to know it properly by this kind of reconnaissance, it would take years, it would take lifetimes.

I am pursuing my old plan and attempting to be thorough, as a capital investment that will bear interest, and am acquiring so much that I can live off it for the rest of my life. Just as people say that nobody who has seen a ghost is ever happy again, so I would say that anyone who has seen Italy and especially Rome can never again be unhappy deep inside. . . .

Now for Egmont and the other things, I don't want to publish anything in bits.*

23. *To his Weimar friends, 13 January 1787*

There's a Minerva in the Palazzo Giustiniani that I deeply revere. Winckelmann barely mentions her, at least not in the right place, and I don't feel worthy to say anything about her.

When we saw the statue and lingered in front of it for a long time, the custodian's wife told us it had once been a sacred image and the *Inglesi* who are of that religion still had the custom of showing their reverence for it by kissing one of its hands, which actually was quite white, whereas the rest of the statue is brownish. And she added: a lady of this religion had just recently been there, had gone down on her knees and worshipped the statue. She (the custodian's wife) was unable to watch such a bizarre proceeding with a straight face, and had run from the room so as not to burst out laughing. When I didn't want to tear myself away from the statue either, she asked me if I had a lady-friend* it reminded me of, that it should attract me so powerfully. The good woman knew only religious worship and love, but had no idea of the pure admiration for a magnificent work, of brotherly reverence for a human spirit. We were delighted to hear about the Englishwoman and I shall certainly go back soon.

24. *To Herder, 13 January 1787*

Here, dear brother, is Iphigenia. . . . I hope it will now seem to you more harmonious. Read it as something quite new first, without comparing, then set it beside the old text if you like. Above all please do anything to enhance the harmony. On the pages with turned-down corners there are lines of verse marked in pencil that I don't like and yet can't now change. I've worked myself so to a standstill on the play. You'll improve them with a stroke of the pen. I give you full power and authority. . . . I'd also like Wieland to see it, who was the first to try and give my stumbling prose a more measured pace and made me realize all the more acutely how imperfect the work was. Do what you both like with it, then get it copied and pass it on punctually with the rest to Seidel, apologies for imposing this burden on you. I myself am a burdened traveller, borne down though not with the curse of the Furies* but with apparitions from the Muses and Graces and all the power of the blessèd Gods.

25. *To Carl August, 13–20 January 1787*

I wait anxiously for news that you are back home and no after-effects are feared, and earnestly beg you to recall me if you feel I am in any degree needed. Though it is certain I could profitably stay here for years, it is also certain that I have already plucked the highest pinnacles of beauty and greatness and can live from them for the rest of my life. I also feel blessed in the psychological effects of my stay. I am more cheerful, open, sympathetic, and communicative. How grateful I am to you for your friendly understanding, and for extending a hand to reassure me about my flight, my long absence, and my return.

26. *To Charlotte von Stein, 17–20 January 1787*

Today I received your letter telling me that my diary has arrived.* How it refreshes my spirit. Nothing since the death of my sister has saddened me like the pain I suffered from our separation and your silence. You see now how near to you I was in my heart. Why didn't I send you the diary from each individual staging-post! I can only say and say again, forgive me, and let us make a new start living together more happily. The shorter section of diary, Venice to Rome, you now have too. I couldn't write any more in Rome. Too great a mass of existence presses in on you, you have to let a transformation of yourself happen, you can no longer stick to your old ideas, and yet neither can you say exactly what the enlightenment consists in. . . .

Thank you for all the news, including the last of the old king.* It feels right to observe a moment's silence when one sees a man like that go to his final rest. . . .

Your letter of 1 January has arrived and brought me joy and pain. I can say no more than that I have only *one* existence, and this time I ventured the *whole* of it on one throw, and still am doing.* If I get off unscathed physically and spiritually, if my constitution and mind and luck all hold and see me through this crisis, then I will make up to you a thousandfold what needs making up. If I perish, then I perish, I was no longer fit for anything anyway.

27. *To Charlotte von Stein, 25–7 January 1787*

I have a letter from Mainz from the Duke, so gentle, benevolent, tactful, encouraging, and cordial that from this point of view too I must seem the luckiest of men. And I will be, as soon as I think *only* of myself, clear my mind of what I have so long regarded as my duty, and persuade myself: that a person has to take the good things that happen to him as a fortunate windfall, not stop to look around, much less ask after the happiness or unhappiness of some greater whole. If there's anywhere that can instil this way of thinking, it's Italy, especially Rome. Here, in a collapsing order, where everyone has to live for the moment, enrich himself, and build a small house again out of ruins. . . .

My great mass of ideas makes writing hard going, for it isn't a matter of single observations and concepts, they hang together, there are all sorts of connections between them, and every day, if I may say so, they progress. I'd be happiest if I had somebody dear to me close by so that I could grow with them and communicate my growing body of knowledge to them as it occurs, for in the end the result swallows up the whole pleasant process, rather as the evening at an inn swallows up all the toil and pleasure of the day's journey.

28. *To Charlotte von Stein, 7–10 February 1787*

Today I spent the whole day drawing. . . . It's taking tremendous concentration to get rid of my petty German manner. I've been clear for a long time about what is good and better, but to find the right thing in nature and imitate it is hard, hard. One can only progress through practice and I don't have the time to work just on a single area. Still, my miserable bit of drawing is invaluable, it helps me with every attempt to picture sensuous objects, and the mind is elevated faster to the level of the general if you look at particular objects more precisely and sharply. . . .

My conceptions of the world are broadening very nicely now, I've seen the sea twice, the Mediterranean and the Adriatic, only so to speak a brief visit, in Naples we'll make a closer acquaintance.

It's all taking a big leap forward at once. Why not sooner! Why such a high price!

29. *To Charlotte von Stein, 13–17 February 1787*

I have your letter and the enclosures, I feel a lot easier now that my friends have more or less given their opinion, so I'm going to Naples for a while, and you'll hear from me from there. . . .

Your letters all get burned at once, though reluctantly. But thy will be done.

30. *To Herder, 17 February 1787*

Thank you a thousand times for your advice and opinion about the Sicilian journey. I won't give it any more thought and just let it happen. I feel every word of your letter about your condition and the women's worries over the children, I would be sad for you in my happiness if I did not see that I'm enjoying on your behalf too and getting splendid feasts of pheasants* ready for you. . . . Hold on until I come back from strolling and ranging, and crouch down again in the old familiar caryatid posture.*

31. *To Seidel, 17 February 1787*

Write and tell me how my account stands. What Paulsen* is holding for me and what's left of my salary up to Easter, also what I can reckon on after all liabilities are met up to the end of the year.

32. *To Seidel, 19 February 1787*

The contents of this box you're to distribute as indicated on the label. Just a word about the seeds you have to pass on to Jentsch. They're all shrubs and trees that can survive the winter in these regions, they'll hardly get through our winter, still it's worth a try. He'd do well to plant the acorns so that for the first few winters they can be covered over. The pine kernels must be put in *individual* pots and kept well in the sun, and also protected from the cold at first, separate planting makes it easier to plant them on, I've even seen that done here. The seeds marked *Diospyros Virginiana* he's to take great care of. It's a very beautiful but very delicate tree.

33. *To Seidel, 19 February 1787*

Banknotes are never honoured here in real money. At most they'll pay out on 10-scudi notes. On other denominations they pay little money and more of their paper. And they harass the customer by keeping him waiting so that everyone prefers to go somewhere else. You now lose $2\frac{1}{2}$ per cent on it. It's thought the total amount in banknotes is 24 million. A national debt that can never be paid off. A short time ago people were losing 5, even 6 per cent. The only silver you see here is Spanish piastres, which they've revalued so that they're worth a scudo, i.e. a full 100 bajocchi, where before they were only worth 96. This operation has immediately raised silver by 4 per cent, which is what sucked the piastres in, but that can't last; as it is they have to rise again, for what are they not worth against paper! Altogether the Papal State is a model of dreadful administration, and now that foreign money is staying away there's bound to be a lot of trouble soon, and then they'll perhaps learn to till their fields.*

34. *To Seidel, from Naples, 9 March 1787*

Arrived here safely and already climbed Vesuvius* too. For information.

35. *To Christian Gottlob von Voigt, from Naples, 23 March 1787*

I could scarcely have had a greater pleasure from home than this news of the progress of the Ilmenau mine. . . . I have only praise for the content of the report. Everybody applies the yardstick of what he would have wanted to achieve himself, and you can best judge the extent of my approval and gratitude if I say that I can't think of anything to add or take away before putting my name to it as if I'd written it myself. I am also reassured over everything you have done and are planning to do about the cable drive and the rest, one is hard put to it to give an opinion from this distance. Please be so kind as to send me news from time to time and reassure me you are well. I take pleasure in the thought of seeing you again and taking up the familiar threads together. Lovely and splendid though the world down here is, one has nothing to do with it or in it.

36. *To Fritz von Stein, from Naples, 20 May 1787*

You would really enjoy the experience of seeing the sea. When you've been used to it for a while, it's hard to grasp how it was possible to live without having seen it, and how you're to go on living without seeing it. I've been right across Sicily without letters of recommendation and without an escort and I've still got through, you can manage anything with a bit of patience and ingenuity. If things work out as I wish, we shall see these regions together some day.

37. *To Carl August, from Naples, 27–9 May 1787*

I look forward to your collection of maps. Now that I've seen one lovely piece of the world, it interests me again in all its parts. . . . The amusing thing about Sicily is that you've no sooner gone a short distance inland before the sea appears again on the other side and a new coast meets you with a laugh of greeting. . . .

The idea of giving Schmidt* the job of supervising the finances has my full approval, he is in every way the right man, I would just point out as a matter of procedure that if you make him Vice-President and leave me with some kind of practical direction, one member of the Privy Council is then subordinated to another, which I think is not a good thing. I would prefer it if you released me from my previous duties with a kind word (and with the usual formula 'at his request') then either made Schmidt the actual President or entrusted the direction to him in the form in which I have had it in practice (though not by the letter of your decree). But I leave all that to you. My only wish was to see you master of your own affairs, anything you do to make them easier for you to manage can only be a source of pleasure to me.

38. *To Charlotte von Stein, from Rome, 8 June 1787*

The last days in Naples I was drawn more and more into human society, I'm not sorry because I've got to know some interesting people. Lucchesini* arrived too, for whose sake I stayed on in Naples the first and second of June. I saw in him a real man of the world, and also saw why I can't be one. Vesuvius, which had been burning since I returned from Sicily, finally produced a strong lava flow on 1 June. So I have duly seen this natural spectacle too, albeit only from a distance. It's a grand sight.* . . .

Yesterday was Corpus Christi. Once and for all these church ceremonies are lost on me, all these efforts to give substance to a lie strike me as shallow, and the goings-on that are impressive to children and susceptible people seem to me, even when I see things from the standpoint of an artist and poet, to be tasteless and petty. Nothing is great but what is true, and even the smallest true thing is great. It occurred to me the other day that a harmful truth is useful because it can only be momentarily harmful and then leads to other truths which are always useful and must be useful, and conversely a useful error is harmful because it can only be useful momentarily and misleads people into other errors that get steadily more harmful. This in the sense of humanity overall, of course. . . .

Incidentally, I've got to know some happy people who are so only because they are *whole human beings*, even the humblest can be happy and in their way perfect if they are whole people, that's something I will and must achieve, and I can, at least I know where the shoe pinches and what needs doing, I've learned more about myself on this journey than I can say. I've been restored to myself, and am only the more yours for it. Death would have been preferable to the life of the last few years, and even at this distance I mean more to you than I did then. So I shall look through everything here that I left behind and then we shall see how things go from there. . . .

Tell Herder that I am very close to the secret of how plants and their organs are generated and that it is the simplest thing imaginable. In these climes one can make the finest observations. Tell him I've discovered the central point where the seed of it all is to be found quite clearly and without any doubt, that I already have an overview of all the rest as well, and only a few points still have to be more precisely defined. The primal plant* will be the strangest creature in the world, which nature herself will envy me. With this model one can then invent endless plants that must all be consistent, i.e. even if they don't exist they still could, they're not just picturesque or poetic shadows and illusions but would have an inner truth and necessity. It will be possible to extend the same law to all other living things.

I very much look forward to Herder's Part Three,* keep it for me till I tell you where to send it. I'm sure he will have made an excellent job of spelling out mankind's wonderful dream that one day everything may be better. And I have to say that I too believe the principle of humanity will finally be victorious, only I'm afraid that at the same time the world will become one great hospital and we shall all become each other's humane attendants.

39. *To Herder's children and Fritz von Stein, 30 June 1787*

The Feast of St Peter was one more time when I wished I had you here with me. Get your parents to tell you what I wrote to them about the illuminations, and anything else there is about it in books. Anywhere in the city if you were high up, you could see the fiery fairy castle on the horizon, and you wished you had more eyes to see it properly. When I'm back, I'll try and give you a real idea of it. Everything is very quiet now all over Rome, and it's a good time for studying. . . . This last week it's been very hot so you don't feel like going out during the day. The nights are very warm too, and as there's a full moon it's very beautiful and delightful. The people are out on the streets all night, especially at festival time, and singing and playing the zither and shouting, and absolutely no one wants to go home to bed. I'm living very quietly all by myself, and as Herr Tischbein is off to Naples, I shall be in a big cool room busily drawing and writing, and thinking of you.

40. *To Carl August, 6–7 June 1787*

I'm working harder every day and practising art, which is a serious business, more and more seriously. If only I could skip a few stages in the *making* of art. I've progressed greatly in the *conception* of it, a genuine hands-on conception at that. Since an artist is after all what I am, it will mean a great deal for my happiness and future morale when I'm back home if I no longer need to creep and scratch about with my small talent but can work with a clear mind, even if only as an amateur. What I'm currently learning is something more that I owe to you, for without your kind message that met me on my return from the south, I would already have left Rome by now. Our friends will have reported that I am extending my stay till 28 August.

41. *To Philipp Christoph Kayser, 14 July 1787*

Instead of coming back your way, here I am writing again, I still don't know how I shall tear myself away from Rome. I find here the fulfilment of all my wishes and dreams, how am I to leave the one place in the world that can become a paradise for me. With every day I seem to grow healthier in mind and body and soon I shall have nothing more to wish for but that this condition may last.

42. *To Carl August, 11 August 1787*

I was waiting for your letter in order to take a firm decision about the remainder of my stay, now I don't think I am being remiss if I ask you to let me stay on in Italy till Easter. My mind is capable of going far in the knowledge of art and I'm urged on all sides to develop my mini-talent for drawing, so those months should be about enough to perfect my insight and practical skill. I'm now working on architecture and perspective, landscape composition and colouring, September and October I'd like to devote to drawing from nature out of doors, November and December to working up the nature sketches in the studio, completing and perfecting. The first months of next year to the human form, face, etc. . . . Yet one more epoch I intend to conclude by Easter: my first (or really my second) period as a writer. Egmont is finished, by the New Year I hope to have finished Tasso, by Easter Faust, all of which I can only possibly do in this seclusion. . . . Completing my old pieces is of astonishing value to me. It's a recapitulation of my life and my art, and by being forced to reverse my present way of thinking and my more recent manner so as to get back into my earlier style and complete what I then only sketched, I'm getting a real knowledge of myself, my limitations and potential. If I had merely abandoned the old projects, I would never have got as far as I now hope to. . . .

If I may add a wish to conclude, it would be that on my return I may be permitted to travel through all your domains as if I were a stranger and form a view of your provinces with completely fresh eyes that have now got the habit of seeing land and world. I would achieve in my way a new image and a full grasp of things, and so to speak requalify for any kind of service to which your kindness and trust may destine me. Should heaven second my wishes, I will then devote myself exclusively to the administration of your lands for a while, as I am currently devoting myself to art, I have long groped in the dark, it is time to get a grip and act effectively.

43. *To Johanne Susanne Bohl, 18 August 1787*

I thought of you when I was in Sicily, how beautifully the wheat grows there and the barley! so to speak in their natural state, how reliable the seasons are and how straightforward the harvest! We in the north seem merely to torment ourselves as wretched imitators. In vain we use effort, patience, and persistence to try and make good what the kindness of nature has not granted us. Many of my comparative observations could be useful. Between Naples and Capua in the same way there is a fertility beyond our comprehension. You only believe the repeated harvests a single piece of land can yield when you see how fast a plant develops here. Last year they took three crops of maize off the same field.

44. *To Carl Ludwig von Knebel, 18 August 1787*

After what I saw of the plant world in Naples and Sicily, if I were ten years younger I'd be tempted to travel to India, not to discover anything new but to see in my own way the things that have already been discovered. I've found what I often predicted, that everything here is more open and developed. Many things that at home I only suspected and searched for with the help of a microscope, I can see here with the naked eye as an undoubted certainty. I hope you too will one day be able to take pleasure in my Harmonia Plantarum,* by which the Linnaean system will be beautifully illuminated, all disputes about the forms of plants will be resolved, and indeed there will even be an explanation for all abnormal forms.

45. *To Carl August, Frascati, 28 September 1787*

I am on the peaceful side of the world, you at the warlike end, and all in all we couldn't be leading more diametrically opposed lives. Here, most laudably, powder is only expended on fireworks and holiday salutes, soldiers are as quick to take cover from the rain as from gunfire. Live and let live is the general motto. . . . Art is a serious business if one goes in for it in a disciplined way, and even connoisseurship is a profession in itself, which people may hardly believe. This much I can assure you of: that if I'd left Rome at

Easter, I positively wouldn't have had the right to say I'd been here at all.

46. *To Georg Joachim Göschen, 27 October 1787*

I can't say that the sight of the three volumes of my works, which reached Rome promptly, gave me much pleasure. The paper seems to me more like good average printing paper than best writing paper, the format shrinks down too much when you cut the pages, the characters seem blunt, the colour is uneven like the paper, so that these volumes look more like an ephemeral journal than a book which is actually meant to last some time. By chance a volume of Himburg's edition* was here, and compared with these it looked like a presentation copy. But all this is now done and can't be undone. In some of the pieces I've gone through I also find misprints and omissions, but can't be sure whether it's the fault of the original copy or of the proof-reader.

47. *To Friedrich Justin Bertuch, 27 October 1787*

Incidentally I'm busy in so many different directions that it sometimes quite makes my head swim. This year has gone by for me like a dream, and if I didn't see so many signs of how much I've gained, I'd hardly be able to convince myself that I've expended such an amount of time.

48. *To Jakob Friedrich von Fritsch, 27 October 1787*

When I came back from Sicily, our most gracious sovereign made known to me views that I could not but devotedly accept, and he has now made arrangements by which the small gap that may have been felt through my absence can be regarded as entirely filled. I therefore hope, with Your Excellency's approval as well, to spend next winter still in Italy and to enjoy the instruction that foreigners are offered from all sides. . . .

With the Roman state, I must admit to my shame, if shame it is, I have not yet much concerned myself. Such bad administration is a sad sight, especially when the ills are so deep-rooted, so entwined with the constitution, that even a succession of the best rulers and ministers would be powerless to cure them. Meantime everything goes along in the same way, the Pope enriches his relatives, puts up obelisks, and distributes blessings as plentifully as people demand.

49. *To Carl August, 17 November 1787*

Egmont is now in Weimar. I take great pleasure in the welcome my friends have given him. I hope you too and others of your rank may find him worth attention, for I should now prefer to write nothing that cannot be read by and appeal to people who lead and have led great and eventful lives.* . . . A word about current affairs, though I can only make out the most general drift of international conflicts. I keep up keenly with the newspapers, and because everything these days comes out and develops quickly, and so much of what used to be done in secret is conducted openly, it is possible for a roving intelligence to see roughly how the land lies. It seems to me disturbing for both friend and foe that France is in such a bad way. On the one hand Prussian-English-Dutch intentions become easier to carry through, yet on the other hand Catherine and Joseph* also have greater freedom of action and can perhaps achieve at the drop of a hat almost total dominance in the south and east while the northern and western powers (in which I include France) are not in agreement with one another. From the Italian angle, I can say that people here privately fear Russia and the Emperor and think that the Emperor cannot in any circumstances favour those grand prospects and intentions of Catherine's on Constantinople unless Italy is guaranteed as a possession for some successor of his too. This much is clear, that the Papal State and the two Sicilies could be taken, like Holland, without a blow being struck. It would only need a couple of ships of the line in the Gulf of Naples and a demand for free access to Rome, and the thing would be done. From various stirrings I believe the Papal and Neapolitan courts are thinking along these lines, though the public has no inkling of it. The people are discontented, the clergy especially, the monks in particular are for the Emperor. Only yesterday a seventy-year-old monk said: 'If only I were to live to see the Emperor come and chase us all out of the monasteries in my last years, even religion would be the gainer.' If Russian ships sail into the Mediterranean and Adriatic, we shall soon see more. Do please burn my letters at once so that they aren't seen by anybody, in that hope I can write more freely.

50. *To Carl August, 8 December 1787*

My heart lights up again at the hope of hearing that you are back home, it revives my wish to be at the place from which really only your absence was at root still keeping me away. Thank you for giving me the news of your expedition,* which has admittedly ended, true to the spirit of our century, in a manner more diplomatic than warlike. . . . I can't do anything but approve that you've given up the idea of completing your set of Rembrandts.* Better to gradually get hold of better prints of the main items. I feel particularly here in Rome that purity, form, and definiteness are more important than that rough vigour and vague spirituality.

51. *To Carl August, 20 December 1787*

The dear little god has landed me in a grim corner of the world. The professional women of pleasure are as risky as they are everywhere. The *citelle* (unmarried girls) are more chaste than anywhere else, they don't let anyone touch them, and if someone makes up to them they say: *e che concluderemo?** For either you have to marry them or marry them off to someone else and once they have a husband it's all settled. In fact, you can more or less say that married women generally are at the disposal of anyone who will support the family. All in all, not a good situation, and the only possibility of a taster is with women who are as unsafe as the professionals. As for the *heart*, it isn't part of the local love-regulations.

After this contribution to a statistical survey of the region, you will judge how circumscribed our lives are and will understand a strange phenomenon that I've never seen so markedly as here, that is love between men. Allowing that it is rarely taken to the highest point of sensuality but stays in the middle range of affection and passion, I can say that I have been able to see with my own eyes the finest examples of what we only know from the Greek tradition (see Herder's *Ideas*, Part Three, p. 171) and to observe its physical and moral aspects as an attentive researcher into the natural world. It's a subject that can barely be talked let alone written about, so it had better be kept for future private conversation.

52. *To Charlotte von Stein, 19 January 1788*

When I hear about your health problems, your toothache, I can't tell you how I feel for you, spending your life in pain under that unhappy sky. I must say that the whole time I've been here I've had no sign of the problems that tormented me in the north and am living here in the best of health and spirits with the same constitution I suffered so

much with at home. There are plenty of signs that I shall leave this
state of well-being behind in Italy, along with so many other good
things.

53. *To Carl August, 25 January 1788*

The main aim of my journey was to cure myself of the physical and
moral problems that tormented me in Germany and ultimately made
me good for nothing; and then to satisfy the avid thirst for true art.
The first I've largely managed, the second completely.

Since I was entirely free, entirely able to follow my own will and
wishes, I couldn't blame anything on other people, on external circumstances, conditions, or compulsion, everything was my own
direct responsibility, and I've got to know myself really thoroughly,
and among my many faults and shortcomings the one you criticize*
is not the least. Living entirely among strangers in a foreign country,
not even having a servant to rely on, wòke me from many of my
dreams, I've acquired a vastly more cheerful and resolute attitude to
life. When I first arrived in Rome I soon realized that I actually knew
nothing about art and up to then had only been admiring and enjoying the general reflection of nature in works of art. Here another
nature opened up, a broad field of art, in fact an abyss of art, which I
peered into with the more pleasure because I had accustomed my eye
to the abysses of nature.* I calmly gave myself up to sense impressions, thus I saw Rome, Naples, Sicily, and came back to Rome on
Corpus Christi. The great scenes of nature had broadened my mind
and smoothed away all its creases, I had gained an idea of landscape
painting, I saw Claude* and Poussin* with new eyes, I spent two
weeks in Tivoli with Hackert* then I was confined to the house for
two months by the heat, I finished Egmont and began working on
perspective and playing with colours a bit. Then it was September, I
went to Frascati, thence to Castello, and drew from nature and could
easily see what skills I didn't have. Towards the end of October I came
back to town and a new epoch began. Now it was the human figure that
attracted my eye, and where previously I had turned my gaze away
from it as from the brilliance of the sun, now I could contemplate it
with rapture and let my eye dwell on it. I went to school, learned to
draw the head and its parts, and now I really began to understand the
ancients. . . . On the first of January I moved down from the face to the
collar-bone, then on over the chest and so on, all understood from

within, I closely studied and thought through the bone structure and muscles, then pondered ancient forms, compared them with nature, and fixed their character firmly in my mind. My careful earlier study of osteology and the body generally stood me in good stead, and yesterday I completed the hand. Now next week Rome's principal statues and paintings will be looked at with freshly washed eyes.

54. *To Voigt, 2 February 1788*

The absence of our gracious master from home is slightly awkward. I await his instructions so as to make plans for my return. Meanwhile I have completely prepared myself to leave Rome after Easter, and already taken a chance that offered to send off my books and all my studies from nature to my mother, my heart is turning towards my friends and from this paradise back into the active world.

55. *To Göschen, 9 February 1788*

I'm longing for our eight-volume edition to be complete so that I can move on to new works. You can imagine what a mass of material I've collected this year, more than I can ever hope to process.

56. *To Seidel, 15 March 1788*

As for Claudine, you lack some of the wherewithal to judge the play really properly. If I've written a *juicy opera*, my purpose is fulfilled.* You're just a prosaic German and think that you have to be able to swallow a work of art like an oyster. Just because you aren't able to read verse, you think nobody must write it.

57. *To Carl August, 17 March 1788*

I will answer your friendly, cordial letter at once with a happy 'Here I come!' Thus are my hopes and wishes and thus is my prime intention fulfilled.

58. *To Carl August, Florence, 6 May 1788*

Now I've got away from the magnetic mountain, my needle again points north; I am here, that is to say: already back with you.

59. *To Knebel, Milan, 24 May 1788*

Now I have a beautiful journey before me. To Como across the lake, to Chiavenna, Chur, and so on. A good deal of granite will get trodden and chipped at once again. I am buying myself a hammer and will strike the rocks to drive away the bitterness of death.

In Rome not a stone was looked at that wasn't shaped. Form had driven out all interest in matter. Now a crystal formation is becoming important again, and a shapeless stone is something. Thus does human nature cast about for help when there is no help left.

EXPLANATORY NOTES

THE TRAVEL DIARY

4 *Lanthieri*: an Austrian lady married to an Italian, a member of the Weimar circle at Carlsbad. G.'s Italian plan was clearly not a total secret. Cf. p. 24.

Supplement a: G.'s supplementary notes, developing points jotted down in the main diary, are to be found at the end of each section (see p. 13).

5 *113 miles*: here and elsewhere I have translated G.'s Prussian mile (= 4.6 English miles).

Fritz: Charlotte von Stein's 14-year-old son. For Charlotte, see 'G.'s Circle', pp. 156–7.

7 *Rubens*: Peter Paul Rubens (1577–1640), Flemish painter and diplomat, active in Italy, Spain, and England; an international figure not only in art. The sketches G. refers to for the Palais du Luxembourg are now in the Louvre.

Archenholz: Johann Wilhelm Archenholz, who had recently (1785) published a guide to England and Italy.

8 *Knebel*: Carl Ludwig Knebel. See 'G.'s Circle', p. 158.

Kobel: Franz Kobell (1749–1822), a landscape painter who had just returned from a six-year residence in Italy.

physiognomic knowledge: G. contributed actively to the work of his friend Johann Caspar Lavater, a Zurich pastor and theologian, on the classification of human types by outward appearance, published as *Physiognomic Fragments in Furtherance of the Knowledge and Love of Mankind* (1775–8). Unscientific though this study was, G. clearly felt it had sharpened his eye for distinctive human traits.

Herder: Johann Gottfried Herder. See 'G.'s Circle', p. 157.

French traveller: Kaspar Riesbeck's *Letters of a French Traveller on Germany* (German edn. 1783) was enthusiastic about Salzburg, but not about G.

threw herself off: in January 1785 Franziska von Ickstadt committed suicide at the age of 17 because of an unhappy love-affair. As the creator of the most celebrated of all suicides-for-love in his sensational novel *The Sufferings of Young Werther*, G. was more sensitive than most in this matter.

9 *Iphigenie*: G. had completed a drama *Iphigenie in Tauris* in prose in 1779, and was rewriting it in verse as part of the completion of old projects that was the main literary activity of his time in Italy.

9 *Haquet*: Belsazar Haquet, author of a *Physical-Political Journey to the Dinaric, Julian, Carinthian, Raetian and Noric Alps* (Leipzig, 1785).

11 *Martin Wall . . . cragfast*: a 1,000-metre-high rock-face west of Innsbruck. Emperor Maximilian I strayed on to it after losing his way when hunting, and had to be rescued. Legend decorously transformed the rescuer into an angel. G. was on occasion, for that stage of the European interest in mountains, a venturesome climber.

Söller to a T: Söller is the roguish hero of an early G. comedy, *Accomplices in Guilt* (1769).

my 'Creation': since 1781 G. had planned a 'romance about the Universe' based on his new interest in science and picking up the tradition of Lucretius (*De rerum natura*). All that remains of the idea is a pair of fine poems, 'The Metamorphosis of Plants' and 'Metamorphosis of Animals' from the 1790s.

12 *dreaming . . . model*: G. was working towards the idea of a 'primal [especially plant] form' from which all actual species developed. Cf. Letter 38 and note.

not got across: G. had stood on the St Gotthard Pass on both his Swiss journeys, in June 1775 and November 1779.

14 *not a specialist*: for all his intense interest and investment of time in scientific observation and experiment, G. was and remained outwardly an amateur. He duly suffered for it in later controversies, especially over the nature of light and colour, where he found the scientific community closed to his empirically grounded questioning of Newtonian orthodoxy.

19 *Etsch*: the Adige. Cf. p. 24.

Everdingen: Allaert van Everdingen (1621–75), Dutch landscape painter.

20 *. . . dit Salomon*: 'Peaches and melons from the south | Are only for a baron's mouth | As sticks and rods are meant to thwack | (Solomon says) the madman's back.' See Proverbs 10: 13.

statistical times: meaning not just numerical but any factual summaries, whereas G. was travelling to get behind such accounts to the felt grain of reality. Cf. his ironic use of the term in Letter 51, to Carl August.

21 *eye is . . . undimmed*: quoting Matthew 6: 22 or Luke 11: 34.

Roos: Johann Heinrich Roos (1631–85), German painter, especially of animals.

22 *assembled Council*: i.e. the Council of Trent, 1545–63, which marked the beginning of the Counter-Reformation.

23 *collapse of the Order*: the Society of Jesus was wound up in 1773 by Pope Clement XIV after being driven out of Catholic lands (Portugal 1759, France 1764, Spain 1767). It was restored in 1814 by Pope Pius VII.

My companion: no companion has been introduced. Perhaps a *valet de place*, a local guide hired for the day.

24 *Adige*: G. has previously called it by its German name (Etsch). He switches to the 'beloved language', as he has just called it, once into Italy.

Lanthieri promised me: the clearest evidence that G. had talked at least in general terms of his plans to travel in Italy. See note to p. 4.

Volkmann: G. took with him Johann Jacob Volkmann's *Historical-Critical Account of Italy*, 3 vols. (2nd edn. Leipzig, 1777), borrowed from Knebel.

... *Benace marino*: '[Shall I praise you, great Lake Como] and you, Benacus, as you stir yourself into waves and a roar like that of the ocean?' Virgil, *Georgics*, ii. 159 f.

25 ... *dove vuol*: 'Down there, help yourself.' ... 'Where?' ... 'Anywhere, where you like.'

26 *frontier*: between Venice and Austria.

Goodfriend: Pisthetairos, the verbally adroit hero of Aristophanes' comedy *The Birds*, which G. translated, produced, and played the lead in for the court in 1780. 'Birds' is henceforth his shorthand for the People, especially where it needs governing (e.g. pp. 44, 73). He gives a fuller account of this adventure in *Italian Journey*.

28 *Voigt study set*: a small portable collection of stone specimens, devised by the mineralogist Johann Carl Wilhelm Voigt (1752–1821).

30 *masters who take it*: G.'s membership of a court and involvement in governing an eighteenth-century duchy gave him a sharp critical eye for social relations and a good deal of sympathy for the exploited. Cf. letter of 17 April 1782 to Knebel: 'I range up through all the classes, see the peasant winning bare necessities from the earth which would be a comfortable livelihood if he only sweated for himself. But you know how it is when the aphids on the rose-stems are fat and green, along come the ants and suck the filtered sap from their bodies. And so it goes on, and we've reached the point where more is always consumed in one day at the top than can be organized and produced at the bottom.'

Pauper ubique jacet: 'The poor man everywhere comes off worst' (Ovid, *Fasti*, i. 218).

31 *Emperor and ... Pope*: Joseph II in 1771 and Pius VI in 1782 were treated to the spectacle of a bullfight.

33 *Maffei*: Francesco Scipione, the Marchese Maffei (1675–1755), archaeologist, art-collector, and a celebrated dramatist, edited collections of antiquities and wrote an illustrated account of Verona.

34 *Raphael*: Raffaello Santi (1483–1520), one of the greatest painters of the High Renaissance, both for his consummate naturalistic skill and for his power to represent ideas allegorically on the grandest scale, above all the harmonizing of Christianity and Antiquity (*The School of Athens* in the Vatican Stanza della Segnatura). As early as 1770 G. had said of works by Raphael that they marked 'a new epoch in my knowledge'.

35 *thought ... about Herder*: Herder had written an essay on 'How the Ancients represented Death', responding to one with the same title by the other leading critical mind of eighteenth-century Germany, Gotthold Ephraim Lessing.

Titian: Tiziano Vecello (1487–1576), leading figure in Venetian art at a time when Venice was itself an artistically leading city.

36 *Marlborough*: 'Malbrough s'en va-t en guerre', the song heard all over Europe since the start of the eighteenth century when the Duke won his spectacular victories in the War of the Spanish Succession.

37 *una doppo notte*: an hour after nightfall.

the Brà: the Piazza Brà, one of Verona's main squares.

38 *Fiera*: the market-hall.

Orbetto: Alessandro Turchi, known as l'Orbetto (1578–1619).

Danae: in Greek myth, was impregnated by Zeus in the form of a shower of gold.

fish from Bolca: fossil fish from Monte Bolca.

39 *Tintoretto*: Jacopo Robusti, known as il Tintoretto (1518–94), pupil of Titian, worked largely for religious bodies.

Veronese: Paolo Caliari, known as il Veronese (1528–88), active in Venice and a collaborator of Palladio's.

Endymion: in Greek myth, a shepherd with whom the moon-goddess Selene fell in love.

Corona civica: the wreath of oak-leaves conferred on the Emperor Augustus for his military and political services to the Roman state.

41 *'dreadfully inconvenient!'*: it certainly could be, as it later was for Wordsworth and his companion on a walking tour across the Alps:

> In eagerness, and by report misled
> Of those Italian clocks that speak the time
> In fashion different from ours, we rose
> By moonshine, doubting not that day was near ...

Doubt set in when it continued dark and they got lost in the woods. See *The Prelude* (1805 text), vi. 620 ff.

Cimmerians: in Homer's *Odyssey*, xi. 14–19, a people living far to the west: 'hidden in fog and cloud, nor does Helios, the radiant | sun ever break through the dark ... but always a glum night is spread over wretched mortals' (Richmond Lattimore's version, New York, 1965).

42 *Ave Maria della sera*: the evening 'Hail Mary'.

43 *Palladio*: Andrea di Pietro della Gondola (1508–80), the leading architect of the Italian Renaissance. Much of his finest work is concentrated in and around Vicenza, where he worked for the greater part of his career. Palladio becomes the greatest single artistic experience of G.'s first contact with Italy, perhaps (if only subconsciously) because he had done in

architecture what G. was now preparing himself to do in literature, namely put the legacy of Antiquity to thoroughly modern purposes.

44 *run-of-the-mill humanity*: the gap between ideal and reality in the theatre is a central theme of G.'s *Wilhelm Meister* novels. The never-completed first draft from the early 1780s, *Wilhelm Meister's Theatrical Mission*, paints a positive picture of what theatre and drama might do to create a truly German national culture, and thus ultimately a German nation. In the version revised and completed after Italy, *Wilhelm Meister's Apprenticeship* (1795–6), theatre is an aberration of the hero's on the way to maturity.

trick the Birds: see note to p. 26.

belittle my friends: e.g. Herder, as a minister of the church.

sorgo: millet.

45 *Three Sultanas ... Abduction from the Seraglio*: *Les Trois Sultanes*, a comedy by Charles-Simon Fanart (1710–92), and Mozart's opera *Die Entführung aus dem Serail* (1782).

Stein: Baron Josias von Stein, Charlotte's husband.

new theatre: theatre was flourishing in Italy. The English rural economist Arthur Young who passed through these regions at just the same time as G. (*Travels in France and Italy During the Years 1787, 1788 and 1789*) was surprised at the number and quality of theatres, some new, that a seemingly none too prosperous economy could support.

Capitan grande: local governor.

46 *Scamozzi*: Ottavio Bertotti-Scamozzi published *Le fabriche e i disegni di Andrea Palladio*, 4 vols. (Vicenza, 1776–84).

47 *St Louis*: Louis IX of France (1214–70).

... at abstinet: 'Marcus Capra, son of Gabriel, who made over this building to his nearest relative [his first-born], together with all his revenues, fields, valleys, and hills this side of the high-road [to Venice], entrusting it to lasting memory while he himself practises patience and abstinence.'

48 *Academy of the Olympians*: a society existing since Palladio's day (founded 1555) for the cultivation of the arts and sciences.

49 *daughter-cities*: i.e. of Venice.

Mignon's home background: Mignon is an enigmatic character with a tragic family history in the novel *Wilhelm Meister's Apprenticeship*. Her famous song of yearning for Italy—'Kennst du das Land, wo die Zitronen blühn?' (Do you know the land where lemons grow?)—set by Beethoven, Liszt, Schubert, Schumann, Wolf, and others, was written before G. came to Italy, but the motifs of art and architecture in its second stanza would exactly fit a Palladian villa.

contact with home: beyond the obvious meaning that *Iphigenie* was begun in Germany and has travelled here with him, there is an allusion to the play's theme: Iphigenie too is alone in an alien culture.

51 *Tiepolo*: Giambattista Tiepolo (1696–1776), pre-eminent decorative painter of his day, often assisted by his son Giandomenico (1727–1804), whose contributions—G. was not alone in confusing the two painters—can be difficult to distinguish from his father's.

52 *Bartolius*: Bartolus de Sassoferrato (1314–57), author of a commentary on Roman law.

foresteria: guest-room.

53 *gentleman*: in English in the original.

sovereign states: Saxe-Weimar was one of some 300 mini-states that made up the political reality of eighteenth-century Germany.

pure: the idea of purity (*rein*, *Reinheit*) had been a key element in G.'s moral and intellectual life for some years. It is too complex and all-embracing to be limited, even in moral contexts, to a sexual meaning. In matters of perception it is close to the idea of objectivity and general validity, but without being so clinically cool.

54 *vetturino*: coachman

Este hills: not so called on maps; the Euganean hills that Shelley's 'Lines . . .' of 1818 were written among.

55 *Giotto*: (1266?–1337), Florentine painter whose work marked the shift away from medieval stylization.

. . . desideretur: 'The image of Cardinal Petrus Bembo was put on public display by Hieronymus Guirinus, son of Ismenus, so that the man whose works of the spirit are immortal may also live on physically in the remembrance of posterity.'

. . . his imagination too: the Cardinal's legendary concern to preserve his style from damage is linked to G.'s own recurrent concern throughout the diary that the mind should be protected against harmful—specifically Christian—imaginings.

to Minerva: Lucrezia Elena Cornara (1646–84), intellectual and writer, gained a doctorate in philosophy at Padua; hence the link with Minerva, goddess of wisdom. She was denied a doctorate in theology—so G. could read in Volkmann—by the local bishop, on St Paul's principle that women should not teach.

56 *Piazetta*: Giovanni Battista Piazetta (1683–1754), a pupil of Guercino, seen as a founder of the late Venetian School of eighteenth-century painting.

Quercin da Cento: Guercino da Cento (see note to p. 93).

Bassano: otherwise known as Jacopo da Ponte (1510–92), painter of the Venetian School.

. . . such a subject: emending the text on the assumption that G. meant to write 'so edel als er *so* etwas machen konnte'.

Salone . . . imagine it: Volkmann said that this grand reception room of the Padua town-hall, at 300 by 100 feet and high in proportion, was the largest room in Europe.

il Bo: the main building—named after the Ox Tavern that once stood nearby—of the university, one of the oldest in Europe (founded 1222). The anatomy theatre is celebrated for its functional design, but G. means 'miracle' negatively, as is clear from the contrast that follows with the Botanical Garden.

57 *Palladio . . . Englishman*: a reprint of Palladio's *Quattro libri dell'architettura* (*Four Books on Architecture*) of 1570, by Joseph Smith, British consul in Venice, whose grave G. there gratefully visits (see p. 77). In his lifetime, Smith in Venice, along with Sir William Hamilton in Naples, was the principal art-collector and scholarly contact for his compatriots travelling in Italy.

58 *Mantegna*: Andrea Mantegna (1431–1506), leading master of the Padua School. The realistic representation G. admired rested in part on the close study of Classical remains. G.'s interest in Mantegna persisted; he later wrote a notable essay on the *Triumph of Caesar* (1823).

without being new to me: far from it. One of G.'s most brilliant early writings is the essay *Von deutscher Baukunst* (*On German Architecture*) of 1772, where he describes how the—then unfashionable—Gothic style of Strasburg cathedral came as a revelation to him. As with Palladio (cf. p. 75), he imagined the architect, Erwin von Steinbach, whispering the secrets of his art and his intentions to him.

62 *Ancient horses*: originally part of a Roman monument, then taken to Constantinople, and finally brought to Venice.

63 *Odyssey . . . Lazarus*: Odysseus disguises himself as a beggar when he returns to Ithaca, to get into his own house and slay his wife's suitors (*Odyssey*, xvii ff.); the story of Dives and Lazarus is in Luke 16: 19–31.

Admiral Emo: Venice was at war with Tunis.

64 *Jagemann*: the librarian of the Dowager Duchess Anna Amalia in Weimar.

65 *scarlet . . . joints*: a bizarre image. *Italian Journey* elaborates: 'in order to make a beautiful statue comprehensible to us'. It is not clear whether this relates to any actual practice of artists or anatomists.

66 *Carità*: Santa Maria della Carità, a complex of existing church buildings to which Palladio added a canons' residence (*convento*), described in his *Four Books of Architecture* (ii. 6). By the time G. saw it, it was not just incomplete but partly destroyed by fire (1630).

67 *Phidias*: Athenian sculptor (b. *c.*490 BC), creator of the Parthenon frieze and related work.

Buffo caricato: a stock figure in comic opera.

70 *Mannheim*: the casts collected and displayed by Carl Theodor of the Palatinate were the main access for eighteenth-century Germans to the experience of ancient sculpture.

pewter dish . . . universe: in January 1600 the cobbler-mystic Jakob Böhme had the visionary experience of seeing, through this humble object, into the 'inmost ground or centre of secret nature'. It is Faust's ambition, in the earliest scenes the young G. wrote of that play, likewise to 'come to know what holds the world together at its inmost centre' (ll. 382 f.).

71 *Wende*: a Weimar servant.

tabarro: carnival cloak.

Vitruvius: *The Ten Books of Architecture* by Marcus Vitruvius Pollio, written in the first century AD and rediscovered in the fifteenth, is the one surviving ancient textbook on architecture.

73 *Sala del Consiglio dei Dieci*: Chamber of the (Judicial) Council of Ten.

avogadori: council members.

oryctological knowledge: in G.'s usage, refers to the origin of rocks.

Astraea: a daughter of Zeus who left the earth when it became corrupt.

74 *Bucentaur*: the Venetian state galley, from which the Doge annually celebrated the city's marriage to the sea by casting a ring overboard.

75 *the fourth book*: i.e. of Palladio's *Four Books of Architecture*.

76 *i imorti! . . . bravi i morti!*: 'The dead chaps! . . . Well done, the dead chaps!'

Felicissima notte!: literally, 'Most happy night!'

Gozzi: Carlo Gozzi (1720–1806), writer of comedies.

al lido: 'to the Lido'.

it was the sea: a notable experience for someone who has been landlocked all his life. He invents a very inland metaphor ('threshing-floor') for its effect on the sand.

77 *children here*: Herder's children and Charlotte's son Fritz.

owe him my . . . Palladio: see the note to p. 57.

Minerva to accompany and support me: in the way that gods and goddesses take on human disguise to accompany characters in the Homeric poems and other works of Classical literature.

78 *Crébillon's 'Electra'*: a tragedy (1709) by the French dramatist Prosper Jolyot de Crébillon (1674–1762).

79 *Bechtolsheim*: a Weimar court lady and writer.

Euripides: G. anticipates the account of this decline given in Nietzsche's *Birth of Tragedy* of 1872.

victory . . . Turks: the Battle of Lepanto in 1751.

Fraternities: charitable associations, also called *scuole* (schools) from the name of their buildings.

81 *Tasso and Ariosto*: the classic—above all, epic—poets of Italian literature. The practice G. describes is one sign of the closeness of high literature to popular culture, something he later tells Eckermann (3 May 1827) he sees in most other nations but misses in Germany.

Rousseau: besides his major literary and philosophical works, Jean-Jacques Rousseau published a collection of 'airs and romances' under the title *Consolations* (1780).

. . . *ben cantato*: 'It's strange how moving this kind of song is, and much more so when it's well sung.'

82 *Santissima Vergine*: most holy Virgin.

83 *Danae*: see note to p. 38.

Sodezza: firmness.

Vaghezza: grace

84 . . . *votre tems*: 'It seems you haven't wasted your time.'

Chiozza: Venetian dialect for Chioggia.

85 *Venice . . . no need to worry*: Volkmann, contrary to more modern fears, had suggested that Venice might eventually be left high and dry.

86 *the Ultramontano*: lands north of the Alps.

87 *Spinoza*: Baruch Spinoza (1632–77). G. returned repeatedly to the Dutch philosopher whom eighteenth-century piety reviled as an atheist. Any heretic appealed to G.'s independent mind, but he also thought he saw in Spinoza's *Ethics* a confirmation of his own vision of nature and emotionally informed commitment to science.

Wieland's . . . 'Satires': for Christoph Martin Wieland, see 'G.'s Circle', p. 157. The *Satires* are those of Horace (65–8 BC).

Goldoni: Carlo Goldoni (1707–93), the great Venetian comic dramatist.

88 *Dessau*: Schloss Wörlitz, built in 1769–73 in the Palladian style by Wilhelm von Erdmannsdorff.

89 *la quale riesce mirabilmente*: 'which succeeded wonderfully'. From Book 1, ch. 28 of the *Quattro Libri*.

l'Inglisismo in Italia: The English Connection.

92 *due ore doppo Notte*: two hours after nightfall.

Tasso . . . misfortune: G.'s play *Torquato Tasso* centres on the poet's fall from grace with the Duke of Ferrara, and is the earliest specimen of what has since become a crowded genre, writing about writers and their problems.

93 *Dido . . . will hold*: when the Carthaginian queen colonized North Africa, she asked for that much land, but cut the hide into strips to enclose a large area. Cf. Virgil, *Aeneid*, i. 367 ff.

picture of Herod and Herodias: by Carlo Bononi (1569–1632).

Guercino: Giovanni Francesco Barbieri, known as il Guercino (born 1591 in Cento, died 1666 in Bologna), pupil of Lodovico Carracci and a major figure in the Bologna School.

94 *Strange*: Robert Strange, an English artist and engraver who worked in Italy from 1759.

95 *Institute*: the University of Bologna, one of the oldest in Europe.

96 *in Delphi*: meant as a sequel to G.'s *Iphigenie in Tauris*, which itself has a powerful recognition scene between Iphigenie and her brother Orest, but the idea was never taken any further. G. gives more details of the plot in *Italian Journey*: Electra comes within an ace of avenging her brother's reported death on the priestess she believes was responsible for it—actually her sister Iphigenie, who has helped rescue him.

Melchizedek . . . mother: cf. Hebrews 7: 3.

Francia: Francesco Raibolini, known as il Francia (1450–1518), a master of the Bolgna School.

Perugin: Pietro Vanucci, known as il Perugino (1450–1523), leading master of the Umbrian School, and Raphael's teacher.

Dürer . . . Alps: G.'s mistake: Dürer did travel to Venice. G. kept his point, if in modified form, in the corresponding passage of *Italian Journey* by saying 'if only Dürer had gone deeper into Italy'.

97 *pheasant dream*: a year before going to Italy, so G. recalls in *Italian Journey*, he dreamt how in a small boat he carried off an immense cargo of pheasants from an island, meaning them as presents for his friends.

daughters of men: cf. Genesis 6: 2 ff.

Guido: familiar for Guido Reni (1575–1642), anticipator of a Classical style that only came to dominance after his death.

While you are attracted . . . to degrade: the whole of G.'s attack on Christian art for its obsession with suffering is carried over unchanged into *Italian Journey*, but the fierce sentence picked out here is missing from the Auden–Mayer translation.

here have to—: what may seem a gap in the MS is present in *Italian Journey* too, as a rhetorical expression of disgust: the angels in Guido's painting *Pieta and Saints* are concerned with a corpse, not with a beautiful living body.

98 *with complete ease*: at the root of G.'s mature writing, his 'Classicism', is the belief in necessary laws inherent in art, with which individual freedom has to be reconciled and balanced. To let subjectivity dominate produces 'arbitrary' results, a key negative term in G.'s classical aesthetics (for example, p. 109). His sonnet 'Nature and Art' of 1800 ends with the lines: 'The master shows himself in limitation, | And only law can truly give us freedom.'

99 *tower . . . built like that*: G. did the Torre Garisenda an injustice; it had suffered from subsidence.

No. 2 . . . No. 1: numbers of rock-specimens. So far on his journey, G. has maintained a single numerical sequence, 1–24 (p. 29), 26–35, omitting 25 (p. 43), 36–41 (pp. 90–1). Here he numbers 1–9, but resumes correctly with 50–4 later (p. 111).

100 *driven out of Bologna*: 'driven' in the sense of 'forced', not 'conveyed by carriage'. G. gives no explanation of what foiled the plan to take the opportune 'coach for Rome' just mentioned. The corresponding passage of *Italian Journey* suggests he later couldn't remember.

101 *wash over larger areas*: in geology G. was and remained a convinced neptunist rather than a vulcanist, i.e. he believed the earth's crust had been shaped by the action of water on it, not by the workings of fire beneath it.

Wandering Jew: a fragmentary poem from the mid-1770s. It remained so.

Ulysses on Phaea: i.e. the story of Odysseus'/Ulysses' shipwreck and relationship with princess Nausicaa, told in Book 6 of Homer's *Odyssey*. The project, under the title *Nausikaa*, got as far as some fragments of text, including some simple lines that evoke the Mediterranean island scene: 'White brilliancy rests upon land and sea, | The fragrant sky unclouded over us.'

102 *the Carraccis*: Lodovico Carracci (1555–1619) was the leading figure of the Bologna School. Also active at the same time were his cousins Agostino (1557–1602) and Annibale Carracci (1560–1609).

Velasquetz: Diego Rodríguez de Velázquez (1599–1660), Spanish painter who passed through Bologna on his way to Rome in 1629 and 1649.

104 *... nella testa*: 'What are you thinking about? A man should never think, thinking makes you old. ... A man shouldn't confine himself to one thing because then he goes mad, he needs to have a thousand things, a confusion of things, in his head.'

Mambrès ... réflexions: 'Mambrès always lost in profound reflections.' Mambrès is a character in Voltaire's story *Le Taureau blanc* (*The White Bull*), with whom G. had apparently been compared.

Duke ... with pleasure: Duke Carl August of Saxe-Weimar had political interests and military ambitions that came to a head just at the time G. went to Italy. Cf. Letters 45, 50.

105 *Ixion's wheel*: Ixion had lusted after Zeus' wife Hera, and was sent to Hades attached to a blazing wheel.

Tischbein: Johann Heinrich Wilhelm Tischbein. See 'G.'s Circle', p. 159.

per non invecchiarsi: 'not to get old'. The slightly abstruse line of thought here seems to be, unlike Don Cesare's point ('thinking makes you old'), that it doesn't worry Italians when things actually do get old, because they simply don't notice it as another nation would.

106 *Maria della Minerva*: as the mixed name suggests, a Roman temple, probably from the time of Augustus, reshaped in the Middle Ages for use as a Christian church.

106 *gallows hill*: St Francis expressed a wish to be buried beneath the gallows.

Bembo: see note p. 55.

between the columns: G.'s description—'cubes, *then* pedestals'—is confusing, because the cube is a major part *of* the pedestal. But his meaning is clear: he sees what the columns stand on not as a series of separate substructures, but as the building's single continuous base (technically the 'stylobate'), which is divided into these separate parts by the five sets of steps set into it.

107 *Kochberg estate*: Gross-Kochberg was the Stein residence, a few miles outside Weimar.

109 *place at Weissenstein*: an elaborate octagonal construction near Cassel.

next four weeks: G. doesn't explain this period of time. It may well be that this was how long he planned at this point to stay in Rome: a first baseline for the successive extensions as his appetite grew with the eating.

Roman history ... happened: aptly, since Terni is where the Roman historian Tacitus was born.

110 *so-called garnets*: garnets cannot occur in lava; these were probably leucites.

LETTERS FROM ITALY

115 *Pygmalion's Elise*: in the Greek legend, the sculptor fell in love with his loveliest creation, and the goddess of love, Aphrodite, brought her to life, as Galatea. It is not clear why G. gave her the name Elise.

116 *his mother*: for Catharina Elisabeth Goethe, see 'G.'s Circle', p. 156.

117 *'mine eye be single'*: see note to p. 21.

serious ... with joy: would be not a bad definition of G.'s Classicism.

118 *Pythagorean silence*: a reference to the fact that this influential philosopher and teacher apparently published nothing.

119 *Winckelmann's 'History of Art'*: Johann Joachim Winckelmann (1717–68) was the first German to write a systematic history of the art of Antiquity. His eloquent shorter essays, especially on the Apollo Belvedere and on the need to imitate Greek art, set going the German fascination with Greece.

tips of your lips: perhaps a positive adaptation of the Greek myth of Tantalus, part of whose punishment by the gods was to be chained within reach of water and fruit, which receded when he bent towards them.

120 *salto mortale*: perilous leap.

121 *diaries ... in the end*: for their eventual arrival, see Letter 26.

122 *genesis of things*: G. here makes explicit his fundamental principle in seeking to interpret all aspects of the world.

123 *amazzamento*: massacre.

Pastore dell'Arcadia: an Arcadian shepherd. The title of the society and its members takes up the tradition of ancient pastoral. This was one of the few occasions when G. was prepared to suspend his incognito.

Megalio . . . mie opere: 'Megalio because of the greatness or grandeur of my works.'

124 *Duke's accident*: the Duke, who was more than a little wild and accident-prone, had suffered a fall from his horse. G.'s strategy of first describing his activities and plans and only then offering to come home is transparent.

125 *publish anything in bits*: G.'s contract with Göschen, and the publisher's announcement, stipulated that the last two of the eight volumes would contain fragmentary works. G.'s preference, despite this, for clearing his desk and conscience by hard work was one element of his Classical phase. The drama *Egmont* was one major task of completion.

statue . . . lady-friend: not yet, as far as we know, the case. But the later *Roman Elegies* do celebrate the two enjoyments, art and love, as activities that enhance each other. In Elegy V, the lover 'sees with an eye that can feel, feels with a hand that can see'. Cf. Introduction, p. xxiii.

126 *not . . . the Furies*: as Orest was, until freed from them by his sister, in G.'s drama *Iphigenie*. Reversing the tragic myth is typical of G.'s positive vision.

diary has arrived: the delay must have played a major part in destroying the already shaky relationship with Charlotte.

the old king: Frederick the Great had died on 17 August.

127 *one throw . . . am doing*: G. uses the same image for his last great crisis, the infatuation in his mid-seventies with a very young woman which produced the great 'Marienbad Elegy': 'I banked on the present like someone putting a large sum on a single card' (in conversation with Johann Peter Eckermann, 15 Nov. 1823).

128 *pheasants*: see note to p. 97.

caryatid posture: caryatids are supporting columns in the shape of (female) figures: an apt image for the bearers of administrative burdens.

Paulsen: J. J. H Paulsen. G.'s banker, based in Jena.

129 *till their fields*: G.'s comments on currencies and state finance are based on his experience sorting out problems of the Weimar exchequer. They point forward to the comic scenes in *Faust, Part 2* where Mephistopheles rescues the Empire from crisis by inventing a paper currency backed by treasure-trove yet to be discovered. See Act 1, scene 2: 'An Imperial Palace: The Throne Room' and Act 1, scene 4: 'An Imperial Palace: A Pleasure Garden' (ll. 5007 ff. and 6037 ff.).

climbed Vesuvius: G. climbed the volcano three times, in increasingly hazardous conditions.

130 *Schmidt*: J. C. Schmidt, a member of the Privy Council since 1784.

130 *Lucchesini*: diplomat in the Prussian service, on a mission of the kind the Austrians had suspected G. was in Rome to pursue.

131 *a grand sight*: on this and the following day, to his chagrin, G. was tied up in farewell visits before leaving Naples just when the flow was developing. But at dusk his hostess, Countess Giovane, dramatically flung open the shutters of an upstairs room to reveal the bay, the mountain, the glowing lava, and golden smoke-clouds (*Italian Journey*, 2 June 1787).

primal plant: the 'Urpflanze', G.'s notion of an original or fundamental plant form that could be directly made out by the eye—his eye, at least— in every individual plant specimen. G.'s later literary partner, the drama- tist and philosopher Schiller, objected at their first meeting that this was an abstract concept, not a perception—which nearly nipped a historic friendship in the bud. In later years G. came round to a similar view himself. Yet his 'primal plant' may still be positively thought of as a model that can be played through like a computer image, with infinite variations and additions. This is very much how G. used it in his poem 'The Metamorphosis of Plants' of 1798.

132 *Herder's Part Three*: i.e. of his magnum opus *Ideas: A Philosophy of the History of Mankind* (1784–91).

134 *Harmonia Plantarum*: 'a harmony of plants', G.'s conception of a botani- cal survey that would complement the *Genera Plantarum* of Linnaeus by going beyond taxonomy to morphology, i.e. beyond the classification of species in separate compartments to their continuity as a single process of development—an early vision of evolution, but with no idea of its mechanisms of genetic change and selection.

135 *Himburg's edition*: ironically, this pirated edition of G.'s works— copyright as yet virtually did not exist—was better produced than the authorized collected edition here at issue.

136 *eventful lives*: the drama *Egmont* (for which Beethoven wrote his great overture and incidental music) is G.'s most persuasive literary treatment of politics. Carl August made a number of criticisms in a letter not preserved. G.'s reply of 28 March 1788 gives, tantalizingly, no precise idea what they were. A nice conjecture of Eduard von der Hellen's is that the Duke took exception to a comment made to Margarete, Spanish Regent of the Netherlands, by her secretary: 'Though you were always satisfied with my services, you never followed my advice.'

Catherine and Joseph: Catherine the Great of Russia and Joseph II of Austria, Holy Roman Emperor.

137 *expedition*: Carl August took part in an expedition to restore the Dutch monarchy after a popular uprising.

Rembrandt: Rembrandt Harmensz van Rijn (1606–69), greatest painter of the Dutch School. At this time, as Carl August's interest shows, his works were still affordable by the relatively humble collector.

e che concluderemo?: 'what shall we agree on?'

138 *faults . . . you criticize*: tantalizing again. This letter of the Duke's is lost too.

abyss of art . . . nature: G. uses the word 'abyss' to mean not, as in modern usage, some unfathomable horror of the world or mind, but a challenging and desirable richness. Cf. Rabelais's phrase 'un abîme de science'.

Claude: Claude Gellée, known as (le) Lorrain (1600–82). French painter of idealized landscapes, lived from 1627 in Rome.

Poussin: Nicolas Poussin (1593–1665), French painter of heroic landscapes, who spent most of his life in Rome.

Hackert: Philipp Hackert (1737–1807), a German artist based since 1768 in Rome.

139 *juicy opera . . . fulfilled*: this is clearly Seidel's simplistic view of the operetta *Claudine of Villa Bella*, which G. is rejecting. Seidel also preferred the original prose *Iphigenie* to the version G. had spent so much of his time in Italy versifying. (See G.'s letters of 15 May and 27 Oct. 1787.) The robustness of G.'s replies is good-humoured. He treated his servant as a reader whose criticisms deserved an answer.

GOETHE'S CIRCLE AND CORRESPONDENTS

Carl August, Duke of Saxe-Weimar-Eisenach (1757–1828). The Duke was returning, aged 18, from the Grand Tour to take up the government of his territory when he met G. in Frankfurt and invited him to Weimar. They took to each other from the first and became friends for life. G. at first joined in some of the Duke's wild goings-on, but gently edged him towards a socially responsible use of his power. They became allies in an attempt to reform the Duchy and make it economically viable: a task ultimately beyond their joint powers.

In the 1780s Carl August looked beyond Weimar and became active in the politics of a 'Third Germany', a grouping of the smaller territories that would be independent of both major German powers, Austria and Prussia. But Napoleon's continental hegemony and his abolition of the Holy Roman Empire and nine-tenths of its independent units in 1806 put an end to that dream. After Napoleon's defeat Carl August gave Weimar a constitution (1816). It was the first German state to have one, and he was the only prince to keep the promise which had been used to rouse Germans against Napoleon in the so-called 'Wars of Liberation' (1813–15). The Weimar constitution provided for freedom of the press (on which the Duke was keener than G. was) and for academic freedom in the universities. In the years of reaction after 1817 the Duke loyally defended both against persistent pressure from Metternich.

Catharina Elisabeth Goethe (1731–1808), G.'s mother, commonly known as Madame Councillor (Frau Rat), from her husband's Frankfurt honorific title, and as Madame Aya (Frau Aja) to a wide circle of her son's friends and contacts. She was loved and taken seriously by all of them, whatever their intellectual or social elevation. Carl August came to visit her when he and G. were *en route* to Switzerland in 1779, and she had a cordial correspondence with the Duke's mother, the Dowager Duchess Anna Amalia. Frau Aja's letters have a vigorous style not a hundred miles from G.'s own, and her forthright and colourful speech must have been as much a factor in the poet's early formation as the maternal love which led Freud to remark, specifically apropos of G.: 'Someone who is his mother's uncontested favourite keeps for his whole life that triumphal feeling, that certainty of success, which not infrequently actually produces success' ('A Childhood Memory in G.'s *Poetry and Truth*').

Charlotte von Stein (1742–1827). A woman of taste and intelligence, seven years older than G. and still attractive enough, after seven pregnancies, to cast a spell on him when he came to Weimar in 1775. Her commitment to social propriety and emotional restraint made her a helpful influence on the bourgeois poet in an unfamiliar court world (Frankfurt was a Free City of the Empire, with no court or nobility). G.'s devotion to Charlotte became total; but by the end of his first decade in Weimar the strain of an intense platonic relationship was beginning to show. The breach on his return from Italy was not final, but the relationship was never again close. They resumed correspondence from 1794, from which point on her letters too are preserved. But they tell us little: it is the earlier ones, which Charlotte had demanded back and presumably destroyed, that would have given us her side of the story.

Johann Gottfried Herder (1744–1803). The most powerful intellect among G.'s early acquaintance, Herder was a (not very orthodox) theologian, an innovative literary critic and theorist, and the influential champion of the distinctiveness of national cultures and historical ages. That made him the father of a new historiography and a modern anthropology—and also, involuntarily, of some forms of modern nationalism.

Herder met the student G. in Strasburg and became a mentor and father-figure. His revolutionary ideas on literature partly influenced G., partly provided a rationale for what G. was already doing, namely creating new modes of poetry, drama, and fiction. When in 1775, having hardly arrived in Weimar himself and against much opposition, G. got Herder appointed as Superintendent of the Weimar churches, it began to alter the balance of their relationship. G. was increasingly the centre of Weimar culture; Herder became increasingly discontented and moody, and eventually a less than reliable ally in G.'s post-Italian literary programme.

Christoph Martin Wieland (1733–1813). An established writer of the older generation who enjoyed great success with his elegant, witty, philosophical-cum-erotic novels and narrative poems in the classicistic mode. He also translated Shakespeare (twenty-two of the plays, but only *Midsummer Night's Dream* into verse). He came to Weimar in 1772 as tutor to the young Dukes—very much a consolation prize after his chances in Vienna had been spoiled by the risqué elements in his writing. But Weimar proved a perfect haven for his later years. Wieland was a mellow personality, a kind of Haydn of literature. One of his most attractive traits was his receptiveness to new young talents, especially G., whose personal impact on the Weimar circle Wieland describes in glowing terms—even though G. had satirized the older man's work. Wieland's sole revenge for this was to become one of the maturing influences and trusted poetic advisers of G.'s pre-Italian decade.

Johann Christoph Friedrich Schiller (1759–1805), poet, dramatist, aesthetic theorist on the grandest scale, G.'s friend and historic ally for the short but intensively productive span from 1794 to Schiller's premature death. They had met in the late 1780s, but began by being chary of one another: G. disapproved of the younger man's wild early works (*The Robbers*, 1782), while Schiller was put off by what he saw as G.'s materialistic philosophy and aloof egotism. But it was a complex love–hate, and at root Schiller thirsted for recognition, after years of hardship, from the man he saw as not just the first but the typologically unique poet of the age. For his part, G. after Italy needed the sympathetic insight and support of an equal. A fortunate chance meeting showed them they had, if not common, then complementary views and talents, and unlikes attracted: Schiller's theoretical and G.'s empirical bent, Schiller's reflective and G.'s compulsive creativity. From 1794 onwards G.'s projects (the novel *Wilhelm Meister*, the first part of *Faust*) benefited from Schiller's radical clarity of mind; while Schiller in his dramatic work (especially the trilogy *Wallenstein*) emulated G.'s concrete poetic vision. They also collaborated in positive harvests of ballads and satirical epigrams.

G. became the key figure in Schiller's aesthetic thinking; while without Schiller's enthusiastic endorsement and collaboration, G.'s Italian potential might have remained unfulfilled.

Carl Ludwig Knebel (1744–1834), G.'s oldest Weimar friend, the court official who, decisively, introduced him to Carl August. Their correspondence contains G.'s frankest comments on the social and political life of a small court. Knebel was a minor figure in the Weimar literary constellation too, as translator of Lucretius.

Louise, Duchess of Saxe-Weimar-Eisenach (1757–1830) was married young—in 1775—and unhappily to Carl August. His rumbustious nature was too much for her sensitivity, and his sexuality too much for her delicate feelings. She bore him seven children, of whom three survived. He had affairs, and from 1802 till his death a recognized mistress, the actress Caroline Jagemann. Observers commented that neither marriage partner could see the other's positive qualities. Since meantime the Dowager Duchess Anna Amalia remained the centre of Weimar society and its culture—which she had been the moving spirit in creating—Louise was left without a role. But in 1806, when the French arrived after defeating the Prussians near Jena, she stayed in Weimar and stood her ground with dignity against Napoleon: 'Two hundred French cannon would not have frightened her,' was his comment.

Philipp Friedrich Seidel (1755–1820), G.'s servant, who had moved from Frankfurt with him. In the early Weimar years something approaching a friend, and during G.'s Italian absence a trusted factotum. He would also venture views on G.'s works and revisions, which the poet was not above responding to.

Johann Heinrich Wilhelm Tischbein (1751–1829). One of the artists with whom G. shared a flat in Rome, Tischbein was his main adviser and guide in all matters artistic. He painted the famous full-size portrait of G. reclining among ruins in the Roman campagna, and also did some more informal drawings of him in their domestic setting.

Christian Gottlob von Voigt (1743–1829). Privy Councillor and administrator, G.'s closest collaborator in various branches of the Duchy's affairs, including the long-running but finally unsuccessful project of reopening the Ilmenau copper- and silver-mines.

Philipp Christoph Kayser (1755–1823). A composer, an old Frankfurt friend of G.'s but resident in Zurich. They collaborated on operettas, but Kayser lacked the major talent that might have established G.'s work in the repertory of music-theatre.

Johanne Susanne Bohl, wife of the mayor of Lobeda near Jena.

Georg Joachim Göschen (1750–1828). Leipzig publisher of the first collected edition of G.'s works, but not subsequently used by G.

Friedrich Justin Bertuch (1747–1822), writer, journalist and general entrepreneur in Weimar.

Jakob Friedrich von Fritsch (1731–1814), nobleman of independent means, Weimar Privy Councillor, and a senior administrator. He tried to resign when Carl August brought G. into the government of the Duchy, but was made to change his mind by a strikingly sensible letter from the young Duke. Later there was mutual respect between G. and Fritsch, but never a relaxed relationship—as is reflected in the style of G.'s letters to him.

BLAISE PASCAL	Pensées and Other Writings
JEAN RACINE	Britannicus, Phaedra, and Athaliah
EDMOND ROSTAND	Cyrano de Bergerac
MARQUIS DE SADE	The Misfortunes of Virtue and Other Early Tales
GEORGE SAND	Indiana The Master Pipers Mauprat The Miller of Angibault
STENDHAL	The Red and the Black The Charterhouse of Parma
JULES VERNE	Around the World in Eighty Days Journey to the Centre of the Earth Twenty Thousand Leagues under the Seas
VOLTAIRE	Candide and Other Stories Letters concerning the English Nation
ÉMILE ZOLA	L'Assommoir The Attack on the Mill La Bête humaine Germinal The Ladies' Paradise The Masterpiece Nana Thérèse Raquin

The Oxford World's Classics Website

www.worldsclassics.co.uk

- Information about new titles
- Explore the full range of Oxford World's Classics
- Links to other literary sites and the main OUP webpage
- Imaginative competitions, with bookish prizes
- Peruse *Compass*, the Oxford World's Classics magazine
- Articles by editors
- Extracts from Introductions
- A forum for discussion and feedback on the series
- Special information for teachers and lecturers

www.worldsclassics.co.uk

American Literature

British and Irish Literature

Children's Literature

Classics and Ancient Literature

Colonial Literature

Eastern Literature

European Literature

History

Medieval Literature

Oxford English Drama

Poetry

Philosophy

Politics

Religion

The Oxford Shakespeare

A complete list of Oxford Paperbacks, including Oxford World's Classics, OPUS, Past Masters, Oxford Authors, Oxford Shakespeare, Oxford Drama, and Oxford Paperback Reference, is available in the UK from the Academic Division Publicity Department, Oxford University Press, Great Clarendon Street, Oxford OX2 6DP.

In the USA, complete lists are available from the Paperbacks Marketing Manager, Oxford University Press, 198 Madison Avenue, New York, NY 10016.

Oxford Paperbacks are available from all good bookshops. In case of difficulty, customers in the UK can order direct from Oxford University Press Bookshop, Freepost, 116 High Street, Oxford OX1 4BR, enclosing full payment. Please add 10 per cent of published price for postage and packing.